Bilingual Families

Full details of all our other publications can be found on http://www.multilingual-matters.com, or by writing to Multilingual Matters, St Nicholas House, 31–34 High Street, Bristol BS1 2AW, UK.

Bilingual Families

A Practical Language Planning Guide

Eowyn Crisfield

MULTILINGUAL MATTERS
Bristol • Blue Ridge Summit

DOI https://doi.org/10.21832/CRISFI9349

Library of Congress Cataloging in Publication Data

A catalog record for this book is available from the Library of Congress.

Names: Crisfield, Eowyn, author.

Title: Bilingual Families: A Practical Language Planning Guide/Eowyn Crisfield.

Description: Bristol, UK; Blue Ridge Summit: Multilingual Matters, 2021. | Includes
   bibliographical references and index. | Summary: "This insightful, practical book can be used as
   a stand-alone guide for families on their language journey, or as an accompaniment to the
   author's successful seminars for families and schools. Learn from the author's extensive
   experience of helping and advising families on how to raise their children as successful bilinguals
   and multilinguals"—Provided by publisher.

Identifiers: LCCN 2020037795 (print) | LCCN 2020037796 (ebook) | ISBN 9781788929332
   (paperback) | ISBN 9781788929349 (hardback) | ISBN 9781788929356 (pdf) |
   ISBN 9781788929363 (epub) | ISBN 9781788929370 (kindle edition)

Subjects: LCSH: Language acquisition—Parent participation. | Bilingualism in children. |
   Multilingualism in children.

Classification: LCC P118.5 .C75 2021 (print) | LCC P118.5 (ebook) | DDC 418.0071—dc23 LC
   record available at https://lccn.loc.gov/2020037795

LC ebook record available at https://lccn.loc.gov/2020037796

British Library Cataloguing in Publication Data

A catalogue entry for this book is available from the British Library.

ISBN-13: 978-1-78892-934-9 (hbk)
ISBN-13: 978-1-78892-933-2 (pbk)

Multilingual Matters

UK: St Nicholas House, 31–34 High Street, Bristol BS1 2AW, UK.
USA: NBN, Blue Ridge Summit, PA, USA.

Website: www.multilingual-matters.com
Twitter: Multi_Ling_Mat
Facebook: https://www.facebook.com/multilingualmatters
Blog: www.channelviewpublications.wordpress.com

The policy of Multilingual Matters/Channel View Publications is to use papers that are natural,
renewable and recyclable products, made from wood grown in sustainable forests. In the
manufacturing process of our books, and to further support our policy, preference is given to
printers that have FSC and PEFC Chain of Custody certification. The FSC and/or PEFC logos will
appear on those books where full certification has been granted to the printer concerned.

Typeset by Nova Techset Private Limited, Bengaluru and Chennai, India.

*This book is dedicated to Maddie, Max and Kate, who have,
in their own inimitable ways, taught me so much about the child's unique
role in their own bilingualism journey
Love you all, Mum*

Contents

Acknowledgements and Thanks ix

Introduction: About the Book 1

The Structure of the Book 2

1 Demystifying Bilingualism 7

The Case for Bilingualism 7
Moving from Fiction to Fact 9

2 Family Language Planning 21

Set Your Goals 21
Creating a Family Language Plan 33

3 Supporting Your Family Language Plan 67

Conversations with Your Children 67
Conversations with Other People 75
Know When to Get Help 88

Concluding Remarks 95

Glossary of Terms 97

Appendix A: Sample Family Language Plan 99

Appendix B: School Planner 102

Bibliography 104

Index 108

Acknowledgements and Thanks

This book has been building in my brain for over 15 years, as I spent time with hundreds of families trying to raise bilingual children and listened to their stories, concerns and questions. Each unique family added to my own understanding of family language planning, and is in some way a part of this book. I thank them all for their confidence in me, and their willingness to share their stories with me.

My own children have been a part of the process, and I thank them for sharing their thoughts and opinions about languages and languaging along the way. Despite the best professional knowledge of 'what I should be doing', I still haven't always got it right with my own children, for which I ask their forgiveness.

And to my sister Erin, who is my greatest cheerleader in my writing, as well as being my time-keeper, coach and copy-editor, I couldn't do it without you. When do we start the next one?

Eowyn

Introduction: About the Book

'But Dutch is a Useless Language!'

When we first moved to the Netherlands I was struck by how often parents talked about not having their children learn any Dutch simply because they perceived Dutch as 'useless'. Some people obviously feel that Dutch is a language with limited usefulness even when they live in the Netherlands. However, even for those staying on a temporary basis, the choice against bilingualism because of the perceived limited usefulness of Dutch is very short-sighted. As a language teacher and specialist in bilingualism, I have long known of the many benefits children can accrue from being exposed to more than one language.

After several of years of getting up on my soapbox and expounding on the benefits of bilingualism – even for a short time, and including if the second language is Dutch – I decided to take my message to a wider population, through seminars on raising bilingual children and with my blog (On Raising Bilingual Children: http://onraisingbilingualchildren.com/blog/). Over the past 15 years I have worked with a wide variety of families, either directly, or indirectly through the schools I work with.

In order to support the needs of families and schools, I have continued to engage in research and to refine and refresh my knowledge about bilingual/multilingual development, so as to provide accurate expertise to the families and schools I work with, and to contribute to the growing body of research knowledge about bilingual development.

Alongside my professional interest in bilingualism I have been doing my best to raise my three children as bilinguals, with varying results. Each of them has taught me many valuable lessons about children and languages, providing both 'aha' moments and plentiful 'oh no' moments. After many years of saying 'No, I'm sorry, I don't have a book', I've finally decided to sit down and put onto paper all the knowledge and work that goes into my Parents as Language Partners seminars and my family language planning work. The impetus behind my parent blog, parent seminars and now this book is to share key information with parents and educators about why bi/multilingualism can be the right choice for any child, and how best to plan for success.

I hope that you will find this book provides you with an understanding of why bi/multilingualism is for every child, as well as how to make it work for your unique children and family situation.

Choosing bilingualism for your child

In many situations, children naturally acquire more than one language through community bilingualism. This type of bilingualism can be perceived as happening almost magically and with little effort on the part of the child. Raising children to be able to use two or more languages outside a community of speakers is much more challenging. Bilingualism is often misunderstood and/or misrepresented in monolingual contexts, and in order to be advocates for our bilingual children we need to talk about bilingualism, we need to know what we are talking about and we need to have a good strategy, with explanations for our decisions.

There are many places along the bilingual road where you may question yourself and your decisions. You may meet other people – professionals or just friends or family – who question your decisions. Your task is to promote the benefits of bilingualism, for your child and for your family, and to advocate for the right help, resources or assessments for your child. You may need to work with teachers who do not understand how your child's bilingual mind works. You may be up against those 'Saturday school' teachers who do not use methods that are sympathetic to their bilingual pupils. You may be opposed by family members who feel that one language is more important than the other. Your best resources in all these cases are accurate information, your dedication to successful bilingualism for your children and your willingness to advocate for them.

I call my seminars 'Parents as Language Partners' because it is a true partnership effort. If you are a bilingual family, it is a partnership between the parents. If your child is learning another language at school, it is a partnership between the parents and the school. If you are a single parent, it is a partnership with other people who spend time with your child/ren. The foundation of a strong partnership is being aligned in your goals for your children and having a clear Family Language Plan.

In this book we'll explore theories and research related to bilingualism and raising bilingual children, determine how to set appropriate goals for your family, learn how to develop a Family Language Plan, discuss how to talk about bilingualism with your children, develop strategies for working with the other adults in your child's life and look into resources and ways to get help when needed. Your Family Language Plan will be a living document that will grow and change with your family's needs and experiences, and you will develop the knowledge and the tools to respond thoughtfully and creatively along the way.

The Structure of the Book

The book is structured in the same way as my long-running parent seminar, as a concise guide that provides both theory and practice. Over many years, and with inspiration from research, practitioners and the unique stories of each of the families I have met, I have developed the six building blocks for success with bilingualism. Each step contains information about a unique part of the journey, and together they form the framework for developing a strong, consistent approach to each aspect of your language journey with your children. For this book, I have taken those six building blocks and created three focus areas. I have included the templates that I use when developing Family Language Plans, and there are integrated questions that I use in the process as well. These two sets of resources will help you understand how to design and implement your own Family Language Plan.

Chapter 1: Demystifying bilingualism

(1) Know the theory

The foundation of the framework is to understand the basics of bilingual development. In this section I have provided what I consider to be the most important basic information that parents need in order to make accurate and realistic decisions for their children regarding languages. I've structured this chapter around the common myths and questions I hear about bilingualism from parents around the world. The aim is not to provide all of the information but to provide enough for a foundation, and the bibliography will give you many further resources if you would like to learn more. In the interests of clarity and flow, I have only included direct academic citations. All of the information in this chapter (and the book) is supported by research, and research links can be found in the bibliography provided.

Chapter 2: Family Language Planning

(2) Set your goals

If the Family Language Plan is going to be a road map for success, it's important to know what the end of the journey is meant to be. Some families have very straightforward goals for their children and some families are much more complex. Whether your family is dealing with two languages or with five, it's equally important to make sure that parents/caregivers are aligned in their language priorities and supportive of each other.

(3) Make a Family Language Plan

Once your goals are set, you can start to build your Family Language Plan. Depending on how complex your situation is, you may have one set plan, or a more dynamic plan which recognises the elements of your life that may change and require a shift in plan as well. This is one of the reasons why understanding bilingual development is important; if your life changes, you will have the knowledge you need to change your plan appropriately as well. There are examples in Appendix A: Family Language Plan and Appendix B: School Planner. Templates are provided, and you can download full-size versions from the Multilingual Matters website (https://vm7. ehaus2.co.uk/multilingual/page/bilfam/)

Chapter 3: Supporting your Family Language Plan

(4) Talk to your child(ren)

For every family choosing bilingualism, part of the process is to have an open and ongoing discussion with your children about bilingualism. Ultimately, the parents may make the choices, but the children have to commit and cooperate as well. It is important that they feel included in the process, and understand the reasons behind the expectations of their parents.

(5) Talk to other key people

Besides the parents, there are many other people who play important roles in children's language landscapes. The job of the parents is to interact with these people and engage their support and cooperation for their children's linguistic journey. Parents may also need to act as advocates if others are not acting in the best interests of their children, especially in terms of language in schooling.

(6) Know when to get help

Raising bilingual children comes with all the challenges and variation that raising monolingual children does, with the added element of concern about language-related development. While bilingualism does not cause language delays or learning difficulties, bilingual children can, like any other children, face challenges related to language or learning. In this section we look at the research relating to bilingualism and special educational needs, and gain insight into when to look for help and what type of help to look for in different situations.

Mother Tongue and More: Talking about Languages

You may have already noticed several variations in terminology in the Introduction, including the terms bilingualism, bi/multilingualism and multilingualism. Although the term bilingualism originally meant only two languages, it is now used more flexibly to mean two or more languages. In this book I will use these terms interchangeably, to ensure that parents feel that their language situation is represented.

Talking about the various languages in your family and community means being able to distinguish them one from another in a way that means something to other people. The most common term in a bilingual context, and the one you've most likely heard before, is *mother tongue*. This term generally refers to the language of the home – the language that a child first learns from their primary caregiver. Traditionally, bilingualism research used the term *mother tongue* to describe the language spoken by the mother. Because there is no use of 'father tongue', there is an implication that the language the father speaks is of lesser importance. Is this true? Is the mother tongue more important? The answer, of course, is 'no'. The language spoken by each of the parents is important to the child, and both should be acquired.

In order to recognise this fact, researchers moved towards the terminology *L1* (first language) and *L2* (second language). For those who were raised as monolinguals, *L1* is the language heard since birth. For those who were raised as bilinguals, the term *L1* actually applies to *both* of the languages heard from birth (or, arguably, from very young). This is also called bilingualism as a first language. For these people, *L2* designates any language learned later in life, at school or otherwise. The obvious drawback of this paradigm is that the use of L1 and L2 or first language and second language indicates a priority system or a sequencing, where one language comes first and the other follows. It seems counterintuitive to refer to two languages as *L1*, or to talk about having two mother tongues, and this can cause confusion as well.

I use the term *home language(s)* to designate the languages spoken in the home by parents or caregivers, from birth. This allows for a child to have multiple home languages, which may or may not be equally important or used, but which share the common feature of being learnt in the home, from birth.

Another term that I will use is *school language*, denoting the primary language of schooling, usually when it is different from the home language(s). The phrase *dominant language* is used to indicate the language in which the child is strongest. This is an important term, as the dominant language will very often change over a child's life, reflecting changes in the languages around them and their prevalence of use. A child may often start with one of their home languages as their dominant language, but over years of schooling in a second language move to being dominant in the school language. I've included a glossary of key terms which includes these and other important terms at the end of the book.

Summary

- Choosing bilingualism for your child/ren requires preparation, continual learning and advocacy.
- You need to be able to talk about bilingualism, which means knowing what you are talking about.
- You will need to have a good plan and clear goals, with explanations for your decisions.

Worksheet 1: Why Bilingualism for Your Family?

Reflect on the questions below to frame your decisions about bilingualism, and your planning throughout the book.

Why are you considering bilingualism for your children? What are your reasons for reading this book?
What are some of the questions or concerns you have about embarking on this path?
What do you feel you need to know in order to make good decisions about raising a bilingual child?

1 Demystifying Bilingualism

This chapter provides an overview of key areas of research and knowledge about raising bilingual children. It is not meant to be an exhaustive overview; there are many excellent books available that are comprehensive and complete. Rather, it is meant to be a bird's-eye view of the field, to help parents understand the breadth and depth of information available about child bilingualism, so that you can decide for yourself what aspects are most important for your family and continue your knowledge journey.

Defining 'Bilingual'

There is a vast range of definitions of bilingualism, ranging from the ability to 'get by' while visiting another country to total perfection in a language. As with most extremes, the truth likely lies somewhere in the middle. The definition I use in all my work comes from a book about bi/multilingual learners in international schools. I use this definition because I think it reflects how all bilinguals, no matter their age, develop their languages.

> Bilingualism is the ability to understand and use two *(or more)* languages, in certain contexts, and for certain purposes. (Carder, 2007: 125, italics added)

From this definition we can see the importance of context, or what academics also call *domains*. Language is learned in a context in which we hear it and a purpose for which we need it. This is the crux of successful family language planning: considering the contexts and purposes we want our children to have each language for, and ensuring that we provide ample opportunities for them to hear and use language in those contexts. As adult bilinguals, our languages will normally still align with this definition; we are accustomed to doing different things with different people in different languages. Switching contexts or purposes for a language will bring a certain level of challenge. Throughout your language planning, keep this 'certain contexts and certain purposes' in mind as a guide.

The Case for Bilingualism

In some of the Western (especially English-speaking) world, bilingualism is still not widespread. But in reality far more of the world's population are bilingual than not. Estimates vary (from 60% to 70%), but no matter the exact number, people who speak more than one language are definitely in the majority. Why are so many people bilingual? In much of the world, bilingualism is a way of life – one language at home, one language in the greater community, and sometimes a national or global (or former colonial) language on top of that. In Africa and India, for example, it would be harder to find someone who speaks only one language than to find someone who speaks many. Yet in some places in the Western world, bi/multilingualism is still viewed with suspicion, especially if the first language (L1) of the child/family is an immigrant or minority language. On the flip side of this, there has been growing interest in having monolingual Western children acquire another language through education, as seen in the rise of immersion, heritage language and bilingual schools. These two facts are a part of a paradox of bilingualism; it is perceived as negative and problematic for some children, and beneficial and desirable for others. Where your family and child fall in this paradigm will surely impact how difficult or easy your journey may be.

Parents making a conscious decision to raise their children with more than one language need an understanding not only of the practical aspects, but also of the background theory underlying bilingualism for children. There are two key reasons to develop a solid foundation in theory and research on bilingualism. The first is for yourselves, as the architects of your child's bilingual journey. Children can become bilingual 'easily' when the conditions are right, but very often it is not as smooth as parents may expect. Understanding the basics of bilingual development, and the forces working for and against a child successfully acquiring a language, will give you the knowledge you need in order to consider which factors require special attention in your particular family situation. For parents raising bilingual children outside their communities, without regular support for one or more of their languages, understanding the benefits and pitfalls of bilingualism is key to success. Those who are mindful of family language planning and consistent in their approach have a better chance of raising a competent bilingual child than those who take a laissez-faire approach. Understanding the benefits you hope your children will accrue will keep you motivated in the face of difficulties.

The second key reason to understand bilingualism theory and practice is for others who you will interact with on this journey. Many families raising bilingual children encounter doubters along the way. Some don't believe bilingualism is necessary, some feel threatened by it and some believe that it is an unnecessary burden on the child and will cause them to have language delays or never to become fluent in any language. Bilingualism is often misunderstood and/or misrepresented, so in order to be advocates for our bilingual children we need to know what we are talking about and how to help others understand our journey with our children. Whatever issues you encounter on your journey, if you have theoretical and research-based knowledge about raising bilingual children, and have established a plan and best practice for your family, you will be better able to counter negativity and not be swayed into changing your plan for your family. Your job as the parent/decision maker is to be prepared and to advocate for your child, and that means having enough knowledge to be confident in your choices.

In this section we will build a foundation of knowledge about bilingual development by examining some common misconceptions about bilingualism and relating them to what research actually shows to be accurate. These are based on the most frequent questions I receive through my blog and parent seminars.

Moving from Fiction to Fact

Fiction: Children are language sponges

Fact: Children, like adults, vary immensely in their language learning journeys

This is one of the most persistent beliefs about bilingualism, and it is potentially very damaging for children. There is a tendency to conflate how infants learn languages with how children learn languages, and presume that what seems effortless for infants is also effortless for older children. In the very early stages of language acquisition (birth to two years), infants appear to have unique capacities in terms of identifying and differentiating languages which are hard to explain without resorting to the idea that they are like sponges. Parents (and teachers and other responsible adults) often presume that this sponge-like capacity endures into late childhood, and make language decisions based on the supposed effortlessness of the process. The reality is that even young children are different in their abilities, aptitude, attitude and motivation for learning new languages. I have worked with many families who put their toddlers into daycare in a new language, fully confident that within a year or two they will be fluent speakers, only to find out a year later that their child seems to have acquired little to no skill in the new language.

There is also variation in how well children cope with being dropped into a situation (daycare, camp, school) where they do not speak the language. Some children thrive and acclimatise easily, some children take longer to settle and, in extreme cases, some children choose not to talk at all (selective mutism). All of these factors show the foolhardiness of expecting children of any age to be exactly the same in their journey to learning a new language, just as we don't expect adults all to be the same. Learning a new language, no matter your age, takes time, effort and the right circumstances – enough input to understand how the language works and a need to use it.

Fiction: Being bilingual makes you cleverer (and a variety of other things)

Fact: Being bilingual does impact the brain, but we don't know exactly how yet, or under what circumstances

Much has been made over the years of the potential cognitive impact of being bilingual, in both the research sector and popular media. Within the research community there is a growing awareness of the limitations of some or much of this early research and a growing hesitation to make blanket statements about how being bilingual affects cognitive functioning. There are so many variants in research on bilingualism that making sweeping statements seems risky. While it is certainly a way to sell bilingualism (and books), the science is not clear enough yet and is being expanded into more precise areas of investigation and research.

The Cognitive Benefits Debate

In the early years of bilingual research (1920s–1950s), the bilingual children who were studied seemed to show delays or development issues, which were attributed to being bilingual. These studies were flawed in many ways, partly because they measured bilingual performance by the yardstick of monolingual performance. In the late 1960s and early 1970s a series of research studies on Canadian French immersion schools turned the tables, and showed not only linguistic advantages but also cognitive advantages for English-speaking children in French immersion schools. These studies provoked an entire field of research, and the attention given to searching for the cognitive advantages of bilingualism continues. For many years, study after study seemed to show that there were indeed cognitive advantages, especially in the areas of executive functioning and long-term brain health.

Over the last decade or so, more critical voices have been heard in the research community about the quality and reliability of the research base. Many of the early studies in fact showed the strongest effect on cognitive functioning for adults, some effect for young children and no effect at all for young adults, but were glossed as showing general cognitive benefits. Complications in assessing studies and comparing studies stem from the widely varying characteristics of the participants, in terms of L1 background, level of L1 and L2 use, measures and tests used and other factors. There is also an issue with consistency in how bilingual and monolingual were defined and operationalised in studies. One of the key areas of research is now linked to ultimate attainment, and is leading to debates around the level of bilingualism that is needed in order to benefit cognitively. This is obviously very difficult to measure, but the principle is that you need to achieve a certain level of competence in a second/additional language for the cognitive benefits to develop.

A further issue is that of a so-called 'publication bias'. In the early years of studying the bilingual advantage, studies showing advantages were more likely to be published than studies that showed no advantages. Certain research groups consistently turn out research supporting a cognitive advantage and other research groups consistently find no advantage. Although more studies showing no advantage are now reaching publication, they are fraught with the same methodological issues as prior research.

The complexity of the bilingual experience and the bilingual mind means that research to date has not been able to find consensus through current research methods. Many researchers believe that the answers will eventually come not from cognitive science research, but from the growing field of neuroscience.

In my seminars and work with parents I prefer to avoid focusing on potential cognitive benefits as I feel they are somewhat of a red herring. Being bilingual has many clear benefits that are as important, if not more important, than the potential of cognitive benefits.

Linguistic benefits

Bilingual children are different from monolingual children in terms of their linguistic development. They are very aware of language itself as something you use and manipulate. Monolingual children develop this at different rates, because they are not confronted with the same linguistic challenges and choices at such an early age. Children who are constantly dealing with two or more languages and mediating between one and the other (for instance, 'I said *kaas* and they didn't understand so I had to use the word *cheese*') are very aware of language, and develop an understanding of how to switch, translate and question to make themselves understood. This makes them better able to talk about language, which give them an advantage in learning language.

The academic term for this ability is metalinguistic knowledge, meaning knowledge about language. Bilingual children know how language works, from experience. They can question why we say things the way we do. They ask things like, 'What's the word for this in my other language?'. They can talk about how language structures are used. As they get older, they understand better how we manipulate language to manipulate meaning because they have more than one way of doing things. For instance, in English you put the verb in the middle and in Dutch you put the verb at the end, which gives insight into how language rules can be arbitrary or contrary. Bilingual children are aware that you can manipulate the parts of language: you can move things around and change things if you want. Monolingual children, on the other hand, have a monolithic view of language: this is just how language is. They do not learn, in the same experiential way, that the rules are different in different languages and that those rules can actually be bent or broken in order to communicate more effectively. The more you think about language and the more you talk about language, the more you can seek out answers for language as well, so you become a better language learner.

Other advantages of bilingualism

The most obvious benefit of being bilingual is that you speak more languages: more languages means more communication with more people. In an increasingly globalised world, being able to interact with others in a common language (and not always English) has immense value in and of itself. For children being raised in bilingual families, it is important that they are able to communicate with members of their family and community in authentic ways. A child who is cut off from the language of their grandparents and other relatives is a child who is cut off from their family and their roots. As parents, we may think that our child may never really need the 'other' language, but we can't predict who our children will want to be when they grow up – they may identify more strongly with one side of their family, or want to explore what it would be like to live in a parent's homeland. Without the language, they are handicapped and will not be able to have those experiences.

In some extreme cases, parents choose (or are pressured) to use a language with their child that they have not mastered themselves. This happens most frequently in immigrant families where the family language is of lower status than the majority language. In these cases, the rupture is not between extended family, but within the nuclear family. This is damaging to the parent–child relationship for many reasons. We pass on much more than language by talking to our children; we also pass on our 'funds of knowledge', which encompass our belief systems, history and culture. If a parent cannot adequately pass these on through the language they speak with their children, the consequences can range from emotional to social and academic.

In addition to communicating with family and extended family, being able to use more than one language opens doors for education and employment. There is growing evidence that bilinguals have more job opportunities and are sometimes even better paid than monolinguals, as well as having better access to post-secondary study. The experience of becoming bilingual helps people to understand the communicative act in a deeper way, and also to understand that people can be different, via language, and yet the same. These are benefits in the workplace, so bilingualism is a hot commodity in the job market. An article in the *Financial Times*, 'The multilingual dividend' (Hill, 2013), explored some of these benefits. Antonella Sorace of Bilingualism Matters was quoted, saying: 'Hire more multilingual employees, because these employees can communicate better, have better intercultural sensitivity, are better at co-operating, negotiating, compromising.'

There are many fields in which bilingualism can be a benefit and lead to employment, pay increases and promotions. In increasingly global and multicultural societies, core services like healthcare, education and social services are actively looking for multilingual employees, in order to meet the needs of their patients, students and clients. Governments and law enforcement agencies are not only recruiting bilinguals, but they are often paying them higher wages. Customer services and hospitality businesses find multilingual employees useful for communicating with customers in their preferred language. International fields like finance and information technology benefit from workers who can contribute to global teams and even lead or manage them.

There is also growing research on the impact on identity development, empathy and tolerance in bilinguals and bilingually raised children. Children who are raised by parents who speak different languages, or in communities where people speak different languages, have natural exposure to people who are different from one another, and who think and do things in different ways. Having access to more than one code for understanding and thinking about the world gives a wider worldview and a more sympathetic understanding of difference. While these types of social benefits are in the early stages of research, I think they are potentially the most important aspect of bilingualism, as they indicate possible far-reaching benefits for society.

Fiction: Earlier is always better

Fact: It depends on what you are measuring

Early and late bilinguals

In talking about bilingualism, an important differentiation is between early and late bilinguals. Early bilinguals are children who are bilingual from before the age of two (approximately), as they are acquiring language for the first time. They are usually learning more than one language simultaneously, either both at home, or one at home and one in childcare. Late bilinguals start learning their second language after the first language has been developed. We also use the term 'simultaneous bilingual' for people who have had two (or more) languages in parallel since birth, and 'sequential bilingual' for people who had one language initially, and added more.

What do we know about earlier versus later language development? We know the human brain is hardwired to learn language, but we don't know clearly yet if it's hardwired better between certain ages. Researchers are still trying to answer this, along with other questions such as whether the brain is more receptive when we are very young (i.e. do we acquire languages better, more easily?). Answers to such questions are hard to tease out. Is it that babies are better at learning language or is it that the environment they are in is better for learning languages? Babies are immersed in language and given extensive input that allows them to acquire languages. We use basic words and simple structures, intonation and repetition when talking to babies and young children. Communicative expectations are low – we only expect babies to say their first word after a year or so! On the other hand, older children and adults are given very different language learning experiences. Often, older learners have little time for learning/studying, but the expectations for success are high. The input they are given is more advanced, as we don't naturally use baby talk with older people.

What we do know is that teenagers and adults are much faster at learning new languages than babies and young children. An adult can go to a language class for the first time and come out of a two-hour lesson able to say three sentences. Older children and adults are better at learning overall, and can use strategies to learn language more quickly as well. When we look at research from immersion education and compare the children who start in early immersion (Kindergarten) with children who start in late immersion (Grades 5–6), the late immersion students will progress much more quickly because they can be active in their own learning process. By the end of secondary school, the differences between children who started in early and late immersion are not statistically significant except in terms of accent. It does appear to be the case that accent is affected by age of acquisition. Many parents cite this when deciding when to add a new language, but it is important to recognise that the potential accent benefit needs to be only one small part of the decision, as it is certainly not the most important aspect of bilingualism, and is not guaranteed just by early exposure.

Is there a 'right time' for immersion education?

More and more parents in monolingual environments are looking for opportunities for their children to become bilingual early. The success of Canadian French immersion schools has promoted the idea that immersion education is a successful way for children to become fully bilingual from a young age. I get asked frequently what the right time is to put children into school in another language, when full bilingualism in the home and school languages is the goal. This is an excellent question, as it rightfully recognises that the home language is important, but also recognises the opportunity to develop in another language as beneficial. Is there a way to achieve both goals? The answer is that there are ways to develop both languages academically, but how to go about it depends on the situation and the languages involved.

Majority Language + Additional High-status Language (Elite Bilingualism)

For children who speak the majority language and are learning a second language, such as in Canadian immersion schools, earlier is fine. In this situation, the children speak a high-status first language that will continue to develop outside school and will eventually be integrated into their education as well. For these children there is no danger of losing their home/dominant language, as both are considered high status. Pedagogically, all the children are in the same situation – all language learners together – and the teachers take this in account when teaching and assessing. For this type of immersion/bilingual education there is no evidence of any potential negative impact on L1 development or long-term academic development, regardless of the age at which children start. This is not to say that earlier is the only way. Extensive research on Canadian immersion programmes has shown clearly that children who begin immersion in late primary school or the beginning of secondary school have relatively the same language outcomes as children who start at the beginning of primary, which indicates that other factors should be considered when choosing a pathway for any particular child.

Local Language/English Bilingualism Through Education

For parents from non-English speaking areas looking towards bilingualism in the majority (local) language and in English, the picture is not as clear. The best option, if available, is a bilingual school where both the local language and English are developed across the curriculum. In many cases this is not an option, so the next possibility would be having children attend a local school for some of their education, and an English-medium school for the rest. Parents often have the belief that starting in English as early as possible is the best option for bilingual development, so children are placed in English schooling from a young age. However, as you have read previously, young children learn language more slowly than older children. They also forget language more quickly, especially if they cannot read and write in the language yet. This would lead to the conclusion that a few years of English education early on may not have the long-term effect the parents desire. If you extend the stay in English language schooling until literacy is achieved, then you are sacrificing the best years for learning the local/majority language literacy in schools.

We know that most children have more successful experiences in education if their early years, at least, are in their own languages. If we consider this as a major factor in our decision making, it would lead us to this conclusion:

- Accessing school in the local language for the early years of primary allows for strong development in the home local/majority language, including development of literacy.
- Joining an English-medium school in the later years of primary or early secondary will still allow for strong development of a majority language such as English, especially as it will be built on the strong foundation of their own language.

Parents will still need to provide support for language development along the way. During the early years while the children are in local (majority) language schools, the parents can (if they want and are able to) start with some social English, either at home through games or reading, or with an English-speaking babysitter. It is not necessary, or even very valuable, to send young children to English 'lessons' – just play with them in English and sing songs and read stories.

After the switch to English-medium education, the parental role will move to helping support continued development in the home language. This can be done by ensuring that the children continue to read every day (and make sure they have access to interesting and age-appropriate books, articles or comics), and by using writing as a means of communication. Writing can be difficult to keep up if the writing system is different from English, but it is very important not to let it go.

A considered approach such as this will work for most children. It is important to recognise that children are not all the same when it comes to language learning, so children who have the same experiences may not end up with the same levels in both languages. It is also important to recognise that there are other factors that are important in decision making. Some children are perfectly fine moving between schools and languages, and take it all in their stride. Other children find change of this nature stressful, which doesn't create a good environment for learning. Language can certainly be *one of the factors* in choosing education for our children, but it shouldn't be the *only* factor.

(Note: In this section I have focused on families who are aiming to develop bilingualism in the home language(s) and English, because this is the situation of most of the families and schools that I work with. The information can be applied to other language situations as well, with the proviso that children who speak English are at less of a risk of home language loss because of the status and availability of the language.)

Fiction: The more languages the better

Fact: Nurturing language development takes time and effort

This particular language acquisition myth exists in part because of the 'earlier is better' myth. Parents who want their children to have the advantages of more than one language can sometimes make the mistake of thinking that children are limitless in their capacity to acquire languages. While it is true that multiple languages are not necessarily a problem, there are limits to what the ultimate attainment will be in each language. The more languages, the less time is devoted to each of them, which affects how well they will be acquired. We don't know exactly how much input children need in order to acquire a language, especially as there is variation among children in this regard. We do know that children need to hear substantial amounts of a language regularly, over an extended period of time, in order to be able to understand and use that language. Children who hear multiple languages in smaller amounts will have more limited skills in each of these languages. It is usual for children to acquire language that relates to the contexts in which they hear it, and so they can have different abilities in each, according to context. This isn't problematic, as long as they are only expected to use the language within that context.

It is, however, important for every child to have at least one fully developed language. They need at least one language that is age-appropriate in terms of vocabulary, structures and comprehension, as a basis for continuing language development and for learning. It does sometimes happen that a child has not had enough input (adequate input) in any language to develop to an age-appropriate level, and this is problematic for learning, and particularly for schooling. Parents need to think carefully about their language choices, and make sure they can plan for adequate input in each of them. Again, this happens naturally in multilingual communities, but for parents raising bilingual children away from their communities a more systematic approach is necessary. It is also important for parents to recognise that children are individuals in language acquisition, as in all things, and that what worked for one child may not work for subsequent children. I have rarely met families in which all of the children are equally successful in all their languages, especially once they have reached school age.

Fiction: Being bilingual means being *equally good in the two* languages

Fact: A bilingual is not two monolinguals in one brain

> Bilinguals usually acquire and use their languages for different purposes, in different domains of life, with different people. Different aspects of life often require different languages. (Grosjean & Li, 2013: 12)

Early research on bilingualism focused on how bilinguals measure up compared to monolinguals. It was understood that the monolingual was the ideal speaker of a language, and therefore a successful bilingual would be exactly like monolinguals in both languages. By this measure, most bilinguals were found wanting, and therefore bilingualism was viewed as being detrimental to development. Although we have for the most part moved past the idea of bilingualism being detrimental to development, the idea that bilinguals should be the same as monolinguals in both/all of their languages persists. This leads to children (and adults) being regarded as less proficient or not 'properly' bilingual if they are not the once idealised 'balanced bilingual'.

In fact, balanced bilinguals are very rare, not because it isn't possible, but because almost all bilinguals use their languages in different contexts and for different purposes, which leads to differentiated development. A child who hears Italian while cooking with a parent will have the opportunity to develop vocabulary in Italian to do with cooking. If the German-speaking parent never cooks with the child, then they may not have a well-developed kitchen vocabulary in German. Bilingual success should be measured by what children (and adults) are able to do in a language in the contexts and purposes in which they hear a language and need to use it. This means that part of the parents' job in language planning is to consider what contexts and purposes they want their children to have for each language, and plan for that to be possible.

Families often face pressure from monolingual relatives about the way their children use language. Bilingual children are all too often measured against the yardstick of monolingual cousins and found wanting. This type of pressure is detrimental to a child's bilingual identity, and may cause them to distance themselves from a language. Positive attitudes and a clear understanding of how bi/multilinguals are different from, but not inferior to, monolinguals is important.

Fiction: Bilingual children start speaking later than monolingual children

Fact: Bilingualism does not negatively affect development

This myth stems from the 'bilingual as two monolinguals' belief. In the early years of development, children who are being raised as simultaneous bilinguals will perform differently in each of their languages. They acquire vocabulary directly from a parent/caregiver, in the appropriate language. In the first years, this means that they will almost certainly have different vocabulary in their languages. They may have some words in both/all languages, but many will only be in one language. As their language systems develop, children start to extrapolate from one language to another and, given the right exposure, they can have the same fluency in two languages as monolingual children have in one language.

Another aspect of this is expecting bilingual children to sound the same as monolinguals in terms of accent. While it is true that young bilinguals have a better chance of having what we would consider to be a 'native speaker' accent, age is no guarantee. Children living outside a strong community of speakers and dealing with other languages as well have multiple influences on their language development. The nature of languages in the brain is that they are complementary, and influence each other, and so all bilinguals may have accents or phrasing that differ from monolinguals. This is not inherently a problem, although some people, especially in education, tend to problematise any language use that differs from their view of what is correct.

Fiction: Mixing languages – by parents or children – is a problem

Fact: Children are more flexible than we think

'Only speak your own language to your child!' is a common decree in much non-specialist advice about raising bilingual children. It's particularly common in writings about the one-parent, one-language (OPOL) method. The reason commonly given is that it is confusing to young children to hear different languages from the same person. This is simply not the case. Children being raised in multilingual communities in places such as India will commonly hear two or more languages from a parent/caregiver, as different languages will be used with different people and in different contexts. What can be problematic is when a minority language speaking parent starts to speak the majority language with their child. It isn't the mixed input that is the problem, but simply the fact that the less of the minority language a child hears, the less likely it is to develop properly. This is a slippery slope, and as the child becomes less comfortable with the minority language, the parent uses the majority language more and more. The advice to only speak your own language with your child can be more helpful for parents than for children, as it ensures that the parents are themselves consistent and don't accidentally drift away from using their own language.

In terms of children mixing their languages, this is also not necessarily something to worry about. All bilinguals mix their languages (also called code-switching or translanguaging) for a variety of reasons. Sometimes we switch for practical reasons – because we don't know a word or because someone joins the conversation who doesn't know the language. Sometimes we mix for pragmatic reasons – because we connect with a word or concept more strongly in one language, or to show our identity within a group. Bilingual language mixing is usually a sign of linguistic mastery, and is almost always done in linguistically accurate ways in terms of grammar. While young children are still developing their languages, they may mix more, for practical reasons. If they have the language skills necessary, they will generally stay in mainly monolingual mode when necessary (with grandparents, for example). If they are mixing consistently in environments where it inhibits their conversation, it may be an indication that they need more input in that language in order to develop to a level where mainly monolingual conversation is possible.

Fiction: Children can't lose their mother tongue

Fact: Children can and do lose languages quite easily

Our final misconception is that children can't lose the first language they knew – what most people call their mother tongue. Many internationally living parents are too relaxed about language planning because they believe this to be true. In fact, young children can lose a language very quickly if they don't hear it enough or if they don't need to use it. I have met many children living abroad who have little ability to understand or use the language they heard for the first years of their lives, because their parents started using English in the home since it was easier. Depending on their age when they moved, some can still understand the language but can't/won't speak it (passive bilinguals), some have limited ability to even understand and some have lost it completely. While this is not irreparable, the older the child is and the more complete the loss, the less likely it is that they will regain it to what would be considered 'native speaker' levels. Even if they choose to learn it again later in life, they may still not attain those levels, or the expected accent. The best defence against language loss is literacy. Being able to read and write in a language gives children the ability to keep growing in a language through the written word, even if the verbal input isn't easy to find. Children who can read and write in their languages grow into adults who have the possibility of continuing to use these languages even outside areas where they are spoken, so it is a worthwhile goal to set.

Through an exploration of some of the common misconceptions about child bilingualism, we have explored different areas of theory. These will be built on in the following sections, to help support understandings of how we develop, implement and adjust Family Language Plans.

Summary: Demystifying Bilingualism

- Being bilingual means being able to use more than one language in certain contexts, for certain purposes.
- On a global basis, bilingualism is more common than monolingualism.
- Understanding the basics of bilingual development will help you to ensure that your child/ren will be successful, and to be confident in your choices.
- Children are different in their abilities, aptitude, attitude and motivation for learning new languages.
- Learning a new language, no matter your age, takes time and effort, and the right circumstances, i.e. enough input to understand how the language works, and a need to use it.
- There are a range of benefits to being bilingual. Some of the commonly discussed benefits are clearly supported by research and others may need further research.
- The languages you choose for your child/ren will impact the approach you take to developing their bilingualism. Having a solid foundation in the home language, including literacy, is often the best start to bilingualism, even when that means starting the second language learning later.
- Bilingual success should be measured by what children (and adults) are able to do in a language in the contexts and purposes in which they hear it and use it.
- All bilinguals mix their languages, for a variety of reasons. As long as your child/ren are getting enough input in their languages, this mixing is beneficial and practical.
- Children can lose languages, including their home/dominant language, due to lack of use and input. The best defence against language loss is literacy.

Worksheet 2: Building a Foundation

What does all of this theory mean for you? It helps you build the foundations for your language planning and for all of the conversations you will have about your child's language goals. This worksheet will help you apply some of the theory and bring to the surface additional things you want to learn or research.

What else do you think you need to know as you embark on or continue your journey with your children? What questions have come up as you read this section that will need further investigation?
Which of the fictions did you believe to be true, and how does the factual information change how you perceive bilingualism and your child's journey?
Does knowledge of the fictions and facts about raising multilingual children change any of your responses on Worksheet 1? Go back and review those questions, adjusting as needed based on your deeper understanding of the theory.

2 Family Language Planning

The exploration of theory in the previous section provides a solid grounding in the facts and fictions of bilingualism. In this chapter we will take this theoretical knowledge and apply it to developing an understanding of the elements of family language planning, and to creating a plan for your family.

Set Your Goals

In this section we will look at making choices and setting goals for your family, for your particular situation. We will examine variables around choosing your languages, look at the types of goals you might set and make some important reality checks – all steps to ensuring that we really know what we're doing.

Choosing Your Languages

There are two main questions to explore as the first step to setting your family language goals: Which languages do you want your children to master, and why? The answers to these questions usually relate to two central factors: the family and the location. Some families come to bilingualism out of necessity – each parent speaks a different language. In these cases, the decision for bilingualism may be simple, even if the implementation is not always easy. Others struggle to find opportunities for bilingualism for their children, particularly in the English-speaking world. Some families are adapting to a new life through immigration – voluntary or involuntary – and a new language is a part of that for the whole family. Additional factors impacting language choices include when one family language is a heritage language, when parents are monolingual or when the child is adopted from another country. In some cases, parents have a plethora of languages from which to choose, as with multilingual mobile families and community bilingualism. What is a parent to do when they have more than one choice of language to pass on to their children? The answer, for most people, seems easy – choose the 'most useful' language, with the gauge of usefulness being tied to outside factors. In reality, though, that is not necessarily the right choice.

The Role of Family

Two parents, two languages

For many families, bilingualism is determined by having two parents with different first languages. It is always the right choice to raise children speaking the languages of both parents, but in practice this is not always what happens.

I occasionally meet adults from bilingual families who were raised as monolinguals. Every one of these adults expressed regret about not being bilingual, and sometimes even greater regret at not feeling a part of the culture of one of their parents. This happens most often with families who have immigrated to a new country – the parents feel that their children need the majority language (often English) rather than a heritage language, and raise their children accordingly. However, the value in a language is not only in being able to speak it in our immediate environment, but to use it as a door into other worlds and cultures. When we live apart from one of our cultures, the easiest access we have to that part of our identity is through the written word or through travelling to visit family. Without the language to do that, people can be left feeling isolated from a part of their own identity.

The best option for bilingual families is that the children should be raised speaking the languages of both the parents, whether or not they believe that it is useful in their current environment. So much is lost when parents do not pass on their language to their children. The most important elements in the shift away from bilingualism are language status and lack of information. When one language, generally the immigrant or minority language, is perceived as being of lower status, there are various implicit and explicit societal pressures on families to stop using that language. I have witnessed this in every country I have lived in, in different ways. The tendency to choose not to pass on a parental language is even more pronounced when a parent speaks a dialect that has a standardised variety used in education. For example, Cypriot Greek parents living abroad feel that 'real' Greek is more valuable to pass on, as this is the status variety that is used in education in Cyprus. The consequences of choosing to pass on a non-familial variety as a priority vary, but in essence the effort is going towards what might be a more globally or locally useful language at the expense of inter-family communication.

Combating this tendency to prioritise the majority language to the detriment of the minority language can only be achieved through the sharing of information. Firstly, every immigrant, migrant or refugee needs to understand the value of the language and the culture they bring with them. Secondly, there needs to be better transmission of knowledge about the benefits of bilingualism. There needs to be a better societal and educational understanding of why bilingualism is beneficial for everyone, to refute the ongoing discussions about bilingualism being a threat. This starts with everyone who works with parents and small children – doctors, nurses, health clinics, social workers, teachers; these people all need a better understanding of why bilingualism should be encouraged, and how to do so.

Monolingual families

Monolingual families are increasingly choosing bilingualism for their children because of its perceived benefits, and this form of high-status bilingualism is usually encouraged and viewed as positive. If you are a family with only one language and you would like to raise your children to be bilingual, how do you choose the second language? For those who are living abroad, the choice of a second language can be as easy as choosing the language of the country you are living in at the time. Thus, I know many families in the Netherlands who are raising their children with Dutch as a second language – a new generation of English-Dutch, Italian-Dutch, German-Dutch and so on. Whether or not this is always the right choice depends on many factors which we will look at in more detail later in the chapter. If you are living in an English-dominant environment and do not have access to a bilingual education programme, finding adequate input to achieve full academic proficiency may be almost impossible. This is not to say that it isn't worth the effort, but being realistic about the results is important. There is a current trend to have language-related baby groups where parents come together with their babies/young children for a couple of hours a week in order to expose them to another language. While there is certainly nothing wrong with that, aiming for bilingualism in this way is unrealistic. If you are committed to having bilingualism as your goal, you will need to be committed to developing a solid Family Language Plan and ensuring implementation across time.

Single-parent families

In single-parent families the language decisions and responsibilities rest with one person. This can be both a benefit and a challenge. It does mean that there is less chance of conflict regarding language priorities and choices, but it also means that it is more difficult to pass on multiple languages. In a straightforward one-parent, one-language (OPOL) situation, the Family Language Plan will be created along the same lines, with only one language being developed in the home. In the more complicated situation in which one parent wants to pass on two languages, the planning needs to consider all elements – time, people, place – very carefully, to arrange for support in one/both of the parental languages. If the parent stays at home with the child, there may be ways to use both languages successfully. While I emphasise in this book that parental consistency is not a prerequisite for success, where one parent is trying to pass on two languages a clear plan for providing adequate input is necessary. If the parent works outside the home, choice of childcare can be critical in successfully developing two languages. As the time the parent has with the child/ren is limited, trying to split it to develop two languages fully may not be possible. In this case, the parent taking responsibility for one language and arranging for the caregiver (nanny, daycare) to be responsible for the other would be a stronger plan. Single parents needn't give up hope of raising bilingual children altogether, but do need to engage their support network in order to have the best chance of success.

The Role of Location

Community bilingualism

Bilingualism, as we have been using the term, tends to refer to individuals and families. Community bilingualism refers to bilingualism in broader social structures, from communities to regions to nations. This type of bilingualism can evolve from many circumstances, ranging from dialects emerging within broader language groups, to the creation of national boundaries that merge different cultures and to the effects of colonialism.

In many places in the world where community bilingualism is practised, people grow up mastering languages that have differing usefulness in different circumstances. For example, in the Philippines most people grow up with a local language or dialect (such as Illocano), the major language of the region (such as Tagalog) and often a third, colonial-based language (such as English). In these types of cases, which language should a parent prioritise? Another example, from the European perspective, is the large number of people who grow up speaking a dialect and a recognised national language, such as Lombard and Italian in Italy or Cypriot Greek and Greek in Cyprus. In all of these cases, parents are generally pushed to choose the national language to pass on to their child. Reasons vary, but it is generally considered that the language that has the highest status is the one to choose. I would argue that while this may *sometimes* be the right choice, it is certainly not *always* the right choice. Language is not only a method of communication but also a means of cultural transfer, and a way of thinking and being. A parent who feels very strongly identified with the culture represented by their minority language or dialect would be better off choosing this language to pass on to their children. One aspect to consider is 'What language makes you truly YOU?'. Choosing a language that you do not identify fully with and embrace may hinder your communication with your children, and in the long run you may regret the fact that they don't share the language that is closest to your heart.

Parents using 'non-native' languages

This connection between language and emotion is often one of the reasons cited for telling parents not to speak a language to their children that is not their mother tongue. The concept of mother tongue is, as we saw in the last chapter, ambiguous, and the idea that the only language you can/should pass on to your children is your *first* language is also incorrect. I am an English speaker (only) by birth, but learned French to a 'native-speaker' level as an adult. Yet I chose to speak to my children in French. I lived in French for almost a dozen years, in Quebec and in France, and for most of those years the main relationships/friendships in my life were in French. I felt thoroughly comfortable and completely 'myself' in French, and I wanted my children to be bilingual and to master both of Canada's official languages. I did, of course, consider the aspects of our Family Language Plan that I could not achieve for my children regarding French, which is why they attended a French school for some years. I've had no difficulties bonding with my children or communicating with them fully, despite the fact that French is not my first language or learned from a young age: other parents can and have done the same. It does, however, require long-term commitment and gets harder as they get older and start to make their own language choices.

Temporary local language

With the rise in global mobility, more families have the opportunity to expose their children to multiple languages over their years of schooling. How should parents decide if a language is worthwhile or not? In my opinion, it is almost always valuable to have your children learn the host-country language, at least to some extent.

Parents frequently ask me 'How long is long enough?' when they are only staying in a place temporarily. Generally speaking, how long you need to stay to make the language worthwhile for your child depends on the age of the child. For children under school age, exposing them to a new language for even a short stay (one to three years) is almost always beneficial in some ways, although the ultimate impact will vary. For older children, the decision needs to be weighed against their educational needs and their motivation to learn a second language.

To begin with, let's consider very young children from monolingual families. Any family moving with children who are under school age should consider daycare/play-school/preschool options in the local language. There are many potential benefits, so if you have this opportunity for your children, why pass it up? At most, they will go on to become fluent speakers of the language and to have some of the benefits of bilingualism. At worst, they will have interacted with people who are different and gained understanding of communication across languages – even if they don't maintain the language after leaving the host country. In addition, it sends a powerful message to children about the value of learning other languages – an especially important message in families where both parents speak only one language.

For school-aged children, the decision is affected by different factors. I have observed children dropped into local schools who have great experiences and come out bilingual in a few years. However, I've also seen school-aged children struggling with the transition to being in an environment where they are not linguistically competent. At this age and stage, much depends on the personality and motivation of the individual child and how well the school supports them. If the child is willing and able, they can absolutely benefit from a few years of school in another language, and if they become literate in the language they have the means to sustain it after leaving the host country. For other children the compromise to their academic achievement, confidence and social skills is too great and the sink-or-swim method is not appropriate. The best-case scenario is sometimes a local school that has programmes in place for language learners and support for the home language as well. In the (frequent) absence of such a school, an international school that teaches in the home language but emphasises learning of the host-country language is sometimes the best option. If no home language school is available, an English-language international school with expertise in supporting language learners would be a good choice, especially if you are likely to continue moving to other locations.

For secondary school aged children, immersion in a local school is generally very difficult. The weight of academic content at secondary school level leaves very little time for learning language to the level that children need to function in academic classes.

Therefore, the best choice again is often a school that teaches in the home language but that also has strong support for learning the local language, or an English-language international school with good language learning support.

Overall, children of all ages can benefit from learning a language that they may not ultimately maintain throughout their lives. For younger children the benefits may be more linguistic and cognitive in nature whereas for older children the benefits may be more attitudinal and give potential for later years, but there is almost always a case to be made for helping your children learn a little bit of the local language on your travels.

Given this analysis, there are several questions to consider when deciding whether or not to have your child learn or go to school in the local language in your host country.

(1) *How is your child doing with the languages they have already?* Are they a thriving bilingual and comfortable with all their languages (or at least with one or two)? Or are they already struggling, either with a diagnosis of some kind (speech or language delay, etc.) or just with language-acquisition fatigue?

(2) *How long will you be in the host country?* Obviously, the longer you will be there, the greater the reason for introducing the host country language. And how many more 'host countries' do you expect that your children will encounter before they are adults? Although children can thrive learning many languages, not all children appreciate having another language thrown at them (rendering the one they just worked hard to learn obsolete!) every two to three years. Living in a culture where you cannot interact with your peers can be isolating for children. As adults we may be perfectly comfortable asking others to speak our language, but that doesn't work for children, who may not encounter peers who can use other languages. Consider their perspective when making language decisions for your family.

(3) *How much does the 'expat' population integrate with the local population?* If you are living on a compound, isolated from the local community, it may be more difficult to introduce the local language in a meaningful way. If you are living in the local community, your children will have more chance to hear and practise a new language, and greater motivation.

(4) *How much time do you have and how much effort are you willing to make to have your children learn the language?* Because it will take time, and you need a plan. During my time in the Netherlands I met many families who just dropped their children into local activities and expected that they would 'learn Dutch'. Often, they were surprised when it didn't work. Putting your child into Dutch swimming lessons and gymnastics classes does not ensure that they will learn Dutch. Some children may be very motivated, and very brave, and learn through attempts at communicating with local children. Many children will feel isolated and insecure and not make any effort to fit in with the Dutch-speaking children at all. They may be drawn to other non-Dutch children in the lessons, or simply be alone. Either way,

it's not likely to be a positive experience that encourages them and motivates them to learn Dutch. You may have better success with a Dutch-speaking mother's helper, a neighbour's child playing with your children, play-based language lessons or other activities where the learning is guided.

(5) *How old are your children?* The younger your child is, the easier it is to find ways for them to be exposed to the local language. Crèche/daycare, babysitters or play-school – all of these are ways to include the local language. Older children need more support as they aren't always confident about learning a new language and have greater communicative needs.

Adoption and language issues: Should our children be bilingual?

This topic came to me through a seminar attendee, and it is a question being posed by more and more families as rates of international adoption rise. Children adopted from 'abroad' arrive in their new homes speaking a different language, and have a great need to learn their new language quickly in order to acclimate and partake in their new family and culture. In many cases these children are considered as, and treated as, bilinguals. But are they in reality bilingual? And more to the point, should they be bilingual? There are, of course, no easy answers. But there are some areas to consider and some things families can do to smooth the way for their new arrivals.

To begin with, most internationally adopted children will not become truly bilingual. If anything, they will be transitional bilinguals, who have a first language which very quickly gives way to the new language. This process of language attrition, or loss, is often called *subtractive bilingualism*, which is when one language replaces another. Most literature on bilingualism tends to consider subtractive bilingualism as negative, with the normal goal being *additive bilingualism*, which means adding a new language and maintaining the old language. However, in the case of internationally adopted children there are often few resources easily available to help support the child's first language, and no real communicative necessity unless the first language is a part of the everyday life of the family. Internationally adopted children tend to lose their first language very quickly – even as soon as three to six months after arrival in their new home they often have little expressive language left. It is not known for certain why this process of attrition happens so quickly, but best guesses tend towards the child's great desire to fit in with their new environment, and possibly also to associated negative feelings about the country of origin (e.g. war or famine) or placement pre-adoption. In addition, the usual complete lack of necessity means that the children do not see the point of continuing with their first language.

There are families who attempt to support the first language of their new arrivals, either by finding a community of speakers or by engaging babysitters or tutors who use the language with the children. This seems to meet with limited success in terms of absolute language maintenance in most cases. However, the message that any support sends to the children about the value of their first language and culture is not to be ignored. Children who arrive in a new country with no language or cultural skills undergo a significant world-shift in a short time. Having no means to explore and explain and question the process would necessarily be an isolating experience, especially for older children. Having the opportunity to use their language to communicate with another child, an adult or a teacher gives them an emotional outlet that they will otherwise be denied. The time frame in which the child chooses to use their first language may be short, but the sense of security and outlet for expression it would provide them could be powerful. So at the least I would encourage parents to try and find someone that their child can speak with in their first language to help with the transition period, and to ensure that the child knows that their first language and culture have value, even as they transition towards their new language and culture.

With no or little resources to support bilingualism, parents of new arrivals can still plan for the best possible transition support. These are some points to consider when making decisions. What do you know about your child's proficiency in their first language? Ideally, you need to know their level of language development in terms of both passive and active language skills, and literacy if applicable. This will help with support at school. There is a difference between getting support for a child who has a language delay or limited proficiency in their first language and who will need intensive support to acquire the new language, and a child who has strong proficiency in their own language.

If you are adopting an older child, what support can you give or arrange for your child while they are learning the language? The answer to this question depends in large part, but not exclusively, on the school chosen. A solid understanding of language development and a willingness to educate teachers and administrators is a good first step. Knowledge of language development is not widespread across our schools yet, so we need to be the ones to carry the banner for our children. Very often internationally adopted children are grouped with bilinguals and offered the same support, but in fact their process is very different from children who maintain their first language at home. Parents can also support learning at home in a variety of ways. There are some good resources available through the Post-Adoption Learning Center, including courses designed to help older children develop school skills (like the SmartStart Program: Helping an Internationally Adopted Child Develop a Foundation for Learning: Toolbox II, Ages 5 to 8 (see www.bgcenterschool.org/CourseLibrary/CL2M.shtml). Other resources may be available through local centres and organisations, especially where there are larger concentrations of children arriving from the same region.

Whatever resources you choose, and however you do or do not support the first language of your newly arrived child, it is fundamentally important to realise that this journey of learning and acclimation is a marathon and not a sprint. Even though many of these children 'seem fine' quickly and thus are perceived to need little support for language or learning, appearances can be deceptive and lack of attention and lack of a support plan in the early years can lead to long-term academic consequences which are much harder to rectify years down the line.

Goal Setting for Language Planning

Now that we have looked at a range of issues around choosing languages for your children, what choices do families have in goal setting? The first decision is which languages and why. The next step is deciding *how* you want your children to be able to use each of the languages that you have chosen. What do you want them to be able to *do* with each language? The strategies and resources that you build into your Family Language Plan will differ depending on the goals you set for each language.

Communicative and literacy goals

Communicative bilingualism is being able to speak and understand a language. A communicative goal is set for languages that you want your children to be able to communicate naturally in: to play, visit and use on a casual, everyday basis. For many families with heritage languages, or with family members who only speak one language, this goal is critical in order for children to participate fully in their community. You may decide that this is the ultimate stage you want your child to reach in one of their languages, especially if you are dealing with more than two necessary languages. This is not to say that they'll never learn to read and write in a language that you set a communicative goal for, but that literacy in childhood is not the goal for this language.

Setting literacy goals for your children means committing to ensuring that they are capable of reading and writing to an age-appropriate level in a language. You may want them simply to read fluently and write competently, or you may want them to master these skills to a level that would allow them to pursue post-secondary education in a language or to work in that language. Another factor to consider when setting literacy goals is whether different scripts (writing systems) are involved. The ideal goal of being able to write fluently in all languages is more difficult, but not impossible, to meet when different scripts need to be learned. Whichever literacy goals you set for your children, it is your job to ensure that the proper resources are available to help them get there. Literacy resources can range from grammar primers to textbooks or tutors; what your child needs will be individual to his or her situation and learning style.

Most bilingual families should set literacy goals for two languages initially. That's not to say that you can't add in others later, but it is important to start with clear priorities that can focus your decisions and actions in the early years of your Family Language Plan. Literacy skills are quite easily (if not always accurately) transferred between similar languages, but the greater the distance between two languages, the more time and effort is needed, especially if different scripts are used.

Overview of goals

For our purposes, it's helpful to combine the above discussions to create three types of goals to use in our Family Language Plan:

- Communicative
- Basic literacy
- Academic literacy

As discussed, setting a **communicative goal** for your child would mean that you are aiming for bilingualism at the level of everyday spoken communication (oral/aural). Your goal is for your child to be able to participate in that language where it is spoken, whether that be at home, at the playground, in shops or when visiting family. This is the most common type of language goal and will be the minimum goal for every language in your Family Language Plan.

In setting a **basic literacy goal** for your child, you are aiming for a functional level of understanding in reading and writing in that language. This enables your child to do things like read the newspaper, write a letter, understand signs and directions and generally function on a day-to-day level in that language. A minimum level of literacy, if at all possible, is desirable for all languages in a child's plan, as this helps guard against language loss.

Setting an **academic literacy goal** for your child means that you want your child to be able to function in school and work environments in that language. This is the highest level of literacy goal and should be selected with care. Most families will set this type of goal for one or two languages. Adding more languages at this level will likely be done only with the full cooperation and engagement of older children, or through bilingual/immersion education or changing the language of education.

What are your priorities and why?

Given the information above, when I work with families on creating Family Language Plans, my advice is to consider language priorities in the following order:

(1) Languages of the parents
(2) Language of schooling
(3) Language of the community (if different from that of the parents and school)
(4) Other languages (foreign languages)

This simplistic list hides other complications, such as parents who speak more than one language each and have multilingual families as well, or situations where there are multiple languages in the community, but it is a useful structure to use when thinking and talking through the linguistic realities of your family and situation.

Reality check

It is important for parents, anxious for their children to do well in school and in the world, to keep their goals realistic. A child who is comfortable and confident in their experiences of languages and learning is more likely to be successful. Moderating our expectations so that our children can meet them while doing well and having fun is more likely to be successful than setting too many language goals for our children. As parents, we must also be willing to do all that is necessary to help our children meet their language goals. This means that we too must do our homework so we are able to provide the resources and support that our children will need. We must understand what we can do to help and have the time and ability to follow through.

Summary: Setting Your Goals

- Deciding which languages you want your children to master, and why, is usually informed by two central factors: the family and the location.
- It is always the right choice to raise children speaking the languages of both parents.
- Bilingual families and monolingual families will each have their own challenges. The important thing is to be aware of the challenges and have a plan to address them as well as you can.
- There can be pressure to choose high-status language(s) for your child/ren. Choosing the language that is key to your identity will help your child communicate with you and keep them connected to their heritage and culture.
- Parents can speak to their children in languages that are not the parents' mother tongue.
- Families that are globally mobile may expose their children to multiple languages. Whether or not to do this for a short stay (under three years) will depend on the age of the child and their needs and motivations.
- Exposing your children to the local language sends a powerful message about the value of learning other languages, and that all languages are important.
- Children adopted from other countries will need support in transitioning to a new language and culture, whether or not they retain any of their birth language.
- Part of your goal setting is deciding how you want your child/ren to be able to use their languages, in other words, what you want them to be able to do with each language.
- There are three types of goals: communicative, basic literacy and academic literacy.
- When setting your goals, consider language priorities in the following order: languages of the parents, language of school, language of the community, other languages.

Worksheet 3: Your Family Language Goals

Using the chart provided, set your language goals for your children. Write on the chart each language you want your child to learn, the type of goal for that language and your rationale for both the language and the associated goal. Make copies of the chart for each child and complete them separately, as your goals for each child may differ depending on the needs of the child, their age when you are starting this plan, and other family or location factors.

Note: the types of goals are communicative, basic literacy and academic literacy.

Name:		
Language	Type of goal	Rationale

Creating a Family Language Plan

What is a Family Language Plan?

In many parts of the world, bilingualism occurs at a community level and is a natural process. In these areas, planning for bilingualism is neither practised nor necessary. However, for families choosing bilingualism in situations where one or more of the languages is not common or not valued, successful bilingualism usually requires planning and persistence.

A basic principle of bilingualism is that children must get 'adequate input' in each language in order to fully acquire that language. This ensures that the child's brain has enough language input to process how it works (grammar) and to acquire enough vocabulary to use the language comfortably. The parents' job is to consider the path of the child, from birth to university age, and decide how to ensure adequate input for all languages along the way. A Family Language Plan is a longitudinal and adaptable plan that follows a child from birth (or later) through to the end of secondary school, to give the parents and child the best chance for success. The process of creating a Family Language Plan helps parents consider their options, prioritise and take the necessary steps to reach their goals. This includes goal setting, mapping out where the input in each language will come from (in terms of people and time), how literacy will be approached in each language and how challenges will be dealt with as they arise.

One plan is often fine for families who are living permanently in one location. Families who move, or who may move, need to have alternate plans or be ready to adapt their plan as necessary. For example, a family who are living in the Netherlands and speak German and Chinese will have an initial plan that is based on the childcare/schooling opportunities available to them if they stay in the Netherlands. If there is a possibility of the family moving to an English-speaking country, they must adapt their plan to continue to meet the goals of German/Chinese bilingualism and consider how they will deal with Dutch, if it was a part of their plan. If there is a possibility of the family moving to Germany, they may also have an alternate plan that outlines their bilingual strategy for the target languages of German/Chinese and any others that were part of their original plan such as Dutch or English. As you can see, the more languages and life possibilities the family are dealing with, the more complex the planning process becomes. Although many families don't formally write down the whole plan and alternate plans, the process of family language planning helps families understand the key elements for bilingual success and the process of resourcing a plan, so that they can make changes as their needs and situation change. A Family Language Plan is never written in stone, but is a guideline and a road map that is flexible when needed.

The benefits of this type of planning are numerous, and include ensuring quality language input in a variety of situations as well as elements such as support for literacy and additional languages. By anticipating the language needs of the children across different life circumstances, the parents have a better chance of guiding their children towards full and functional bilingualism.

Is it hard to raise a successful bilingual in this way? Some families do it more easily than others and some languages are easier to support. Families dealing with a need for three or more languages, or families who move often, need to think carefully about what their language priorities are and how they will reach those goals, and have a clear plan. This gives their children the best chance for success on their bilingual journey.

Elements of a Family Language Plan

The Family Language Plan process considers the following factors:

- *Language goals:* Once the goals for each language involved have been set, these will be the basis of the Family Language Plan.
- *People:* What people will be critical in helping the children achieve bilingualism, and what do the parents need to consider in terms of their roles and the roles of other people involved in the family structure?
- *Phases of life:* A plan should include specific information for each phase – early years, primary school, secondary school – as needs and opportunities will vary by age and stage.
- *Resources:* What resources will be needed to support all the languages in the Family Language Plan? How will these resources change if the family moves schools/country or other?

Planning for input: How much is 'enough'?

Whether you are an expat family considering a new local language for your children or a family dealing with multiple languages, the concern about amount of language is the same. How much of a language, over what time frame, is *enough* for bilingualism to be successful? Or, at the least, how much is enough to make it worthwhile for the parents and the children? This is a complex question and there is no clear answer coming from research. Many researchers use a guideline of a minimum of 20% of the least-used language as a benchmark for finding bilingual children to study, which would indicate that this would be the lowest amount that would lead to bilingualism. This threshold is hotly contested by some on the internet and it is true that it is not a firm number. In my experience of working with families, with 20% input in a language the children are generally passive bilinguals; they may understand the language fairly well but they will rarely, if ever, use it voluntarily. This is perfectly normal: if the child has a language they are much stronger in (or two languages), they will default to these whenever possible. Even bilingual adults struggle to use a weaker language if they don't really need to in their environment.

The answer to how much input is enough is also related to what goals you have set for different languages. If you are aiming only for verbal communication (speaking, listening) for a language, this is easier to achieve than academic proficiency. For example, if you only want your child to be able to talk to their grandparents once a year, the amount of input needed to develop that level of ability is vastly different from a language you envision your child attending university in one day. This is one of the reasons why goal setting and planning is so important; without an idea of where you are heading it is all too easy to end up far off track.

There is also a difference between a lot of lower-quality input, and higher-quality input in lesser amounts. The type of language we tend to use at home with our children is restricted, repetitive and often more about getting things done than developing language. In our day-to-day interactions we may use the same kind of language around the same topics in most of our communication with our children. This type of input is not particularly rich for language development, and does not necessarily promote advanced vocabulary development or increasingly complex structures. I often meet adults that were raised in bilingual families who feel that they sound child-like in the minority language because their level of language never quite developed past a basic level in terms of conversational ability. This is the type of language that develops at home if we don't pay attention to enriching language rather than just everyday communication. If there is a language that you know does not get robust input, increasing the quality of that input is a good way to aim for better development. This can be done through reading, game playing, discussing school topics and other cognitively challenging activities.

There are also clearly some kinds of language input that lead to language development and some that don't or that are limited. When we talk about input for language learning, we mean speech directed to a baby/child by a person. The amount of talking that a baby hears is predictive of where they are going to end up in terms of language development, and needs to be maximised in each important language. In the early years, other sources such as television, apps, etc. have little to no impact on language acquisition. One-on-one activities provide young children with the best quality language input, and will lead to the greatest language gains.

Considering Language Input for Your Family Language Plan

There are three factors that you need to consider when making the decision about what is 'enough' for the languages in your language plan.

The first is the age of the child when starting with the language. If you are starting when your child is born you have many years to provide consistent input, and so if progress is sometimes slow you can readjust and help pick it up again. While it is not true that younger children are *faster* language learners, it is true that they simply have more time ahead of them to develop. If you are adding in another language when your child is older and aiming for a literacy goal, then you will need to ensure enough input to help them progress quickly.

The second factor to consider is your language goals. If you want your child to be a fluent speaker of a language and to be able to read and write in it, then 'enough' is going to be a serious commitment in any language other than the language of schooling. Most families find that they can manage enough input in two languages to achieve this level in both, but the more languages you include the harder it becomes to find the time (and energy!) to provide adequate, good-quality input. When looking at your family situation, then, you plan for the amount of input that will help your children reach your language goals. If you have a minority language spoken at home and want your children to be able to understand it, you may be able to get away with a couple of hours every day. If you speak a minority language at home but would like your children to be able to go home to your country to university some day, the time and effort needed to develop the language to that level will be much greater (for the parents and the children).

The third factor you need to consider is the individual child. We have established that children are not linguistic sponges and that there is much variation between children in terms of aptitude, attitude and motivation. This means that each child's personality and linguistic characteristics must be considered as a part of the decision-making process, and the outcomes will likely not be the same for all children in a family.

Mapping Input

Mapping language input is not straightforward, and is certainly not a scientifically precise process. Over the years I have found that the best way to visualise the language balance for your child is to map where they are over each day, and what language(s) would be spoken to them in that environment. For example, if your child is in an English-speaking school, you map the school hours as mainly English input. If your home is bilingual, you map time at home in both languages. While this mapping system will not give you an exact amount of input per language, it will give you an overview and will often reveal surprising language patterns, especially in terms of how little minority language exposure children get. Once the chart is completed, the results can be compared with the language goals that have been set, to check if the two elements are aligned or mismatched. This mapping exercise can be done whenever there is a change in language use (new babysitter, etc.) or if you are concerned that a language is not developing as you would wish. Often a quick input map (e.g. Figure 2.1) will give you a picture of what needs changing.

In some cases this type of language map will not be representative for various reasons. For some families the input amounts change significantly at different times of the year. If one parent speaks the majority language and the other parent speaks a minority language that is not well represented in their environment, there can be a serious imbalance in language input on a day-to-day basis. If resources for the minority language are not available, taking children to visit minority language speaking families during the holidays can provide them with an input flood to regain fluency in the language. For example, a Dutch-Portuguese family living in the Netherlands will find that Dutch is dominant in that environment. If the children go to Portugal for the summer for two months and are immersed in Portuguese, their Portuguese will improve significantly.

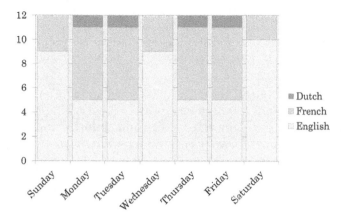

Figure 2.1 Example of a language input map

When they return to the Netherlands it will dwindle again, until the next visit to Portugal at Christmas. This method isn't ideal, as it can be hard work for the children to live through repeated immersion experiences, but for some families this is the best avenue open to them.

In families where both parents speak both/all languages, language use in the home can be so dynamic as to be impossible to quantify. Families that have translanguaging as their main means of communication engage in such dynamic use of language that it can't be boxed up on a chart. There is no problem with this approach as long as parents are happy to have the children take the lead on language development. If a significant imbalance is developing, the parents need to consider if they are willing to accept this or if they want to adapt their approach to be more explicit in developing the language that is lagging.

Planning for Simultaneous Bilingualism

There are a variety of recognised methods for promoting the development of simultaneous bilingualism from birth (or very young). Some are more common in bilingual families, and some in families that speak a language (or languages) that are different from the community they live in. The following is a brief overview of the types and practices associated with them.

Simultaneous bilingualism approaches

- One-parent, one-language (OPOL)
- Minority language at home (MLaH)
- Domains of use

One-parent, one-language (OPOL)

> OPOL is not a guaranteed method of success as there are many other factors (e.g. in the community) that affect language development in childhood and not least in the teenage years. (Baker, 2014: 17)

The OPOL approach is probably the most well-known and written-about approach to family bilingualism. It sounds very straightforward, in that the basic requirement is that each parent speaks their own language to the child/children, exclusively. So I speak French to my children and my husband speaks English to them, and they will grow up bilingual. But the reality, as with anything to do with families or children, is not as simple or as clear cut.

Just employing the OPOL method can sometimes produce the necessary conditions for bilingualism, but over my years of working with bilingual families I have observed that it doesn't guarantee success. Here are what I find to be the most common complications or limitations of OPOL:

(1) *Lack of minority language development.* Many couples are in a situation where one parent speaks the majority language of the community and the other parent speaks a minority language. Realistically, their children are going to grow up hearing more of the majority language, because it surrounds them. By the time the children are in school (or earlier if they are in childcare in the majority language) they will be spending most of their time in the majority language, especially if the minority language speaking parent works full time. In situations like this where there is a clear and significant imbalance of input, it is clear that the minority language will struggle to develop.

(2) *Slide towards the majority language.* In many bilingual families, the minority language speaking partner also speaks the majority language. This happens frequently in the English-speaking world (or other immigrant paradigms) where, for example, a Spanish/English-speaking American marries an English-speaking American. Often, the Spanish-speaking parent sets out with the best of intentions, determined to pass on Spanish to the children. But then they use a lot of English too, to be inclusive with friends and family and to talk to child minders/teachers ... and the children very quickly pick up on the fact that Spanish is not *necessary* to communicate with that parent, or with anyone. They can use English all the time, and be just fine. So the children start speaking to the parent in English, and while the parent makes a valiant effort to keep speaking Spanish, eventually the use of Spanish dwindles ... and the children are not bilingual at all, or any more.

(3) *Lack of consistency in working towards language goals.* Sometimes a parent who speaks both languages (and possibly other languages too) in an OPOL family can have problems with choosing what language to speak, so they use a little of this and a little of that. A lot of the OPOL literature stresses consistency, and although it isn't necessary from the children's perspective, it does help the adults to be more sure of providing the input that is needed. Also, the early years are the time when the parents

have the most influence over their children, so if you are passing on a minority language it's important to use these years to transmit as much language you can. It may well happen that eventually people slide towards the majority language, but if you did a great job of building a language foundation before your children start to use only the majority language, they have a better chance of coming back to the language later.

OPOL: The minority language dilemma

... the minority language needs care and attention, status and much usage in the young child. (Baker & Wright, 2017: 120)

The reality is that it's a hard job being the minority language parent, no matter what that language may be. But if the minority language is a lesser-spoken language, or if it is the language of a working parent, who naturally has less time to spend speaking to the children, the job becomes harder still. So, if you are the minority language parent or you are a parent who works or travels a lot, should you give up your hope that your children will be fluent in your language? The answer is 'Of course not!'. But how do you make that work?

Take the example of a Russian-speaking mother, raising her children with her Dutch-speaking partner in the Netherlands. How can this parent ensure enough Russian input and also promote Russian as a useful language to her children? In this case, in the early years, Russian may be the children's language of choice – it is the language spoken to them by their primary caregiver, all day, every day. Dad is there in the evenings and at weekends with his Dutch, and the children are likely happy to use both languages at this point. But what happens when the children start childcare or school, and then are living in Dutch for the majority of their language-learning hours? Unfortunately, many children at this point go through a phase of only wanting to use the majority language (in this case, Dutch) and refusing to use the minority language. This is especially true if the minority language parent also speaks the majority language. So, what's a parent to do? There are many small steps to take in attempting to maintain a minority language.

The first factor is to find your child's currency – what are they really interested in? What will motivate them to use the minority language? For some children, this means a hobby that they can only access in the minority language, or creating a community of practice based on common interests or even having certain resources (books, DVDs, computer games) only available in the minority language. The point is to continue to show the child that the minority language is a useful, living language, and that they *need* it to accomplish something that is important to them.

A second important element of increasing minority language use is to find other speakers of the language to participate in the children's lives. If at all possible, parents should surround themselves with friends and household help that speak the minority language, and encourage them to speak to the children. This could be through formal childcare, but it can also be accomplished by hiring a minority language speaking teenager to come and play with the children a few times a week (or more!). Visits to family are invaluable, and should be undertaken as often as possible – it can be hard to motivate a child in Amsterdam to speak Russian, but that same child may blossom in Moscow.

The bottom line is that a minority language parent has a hard job, and one that cannot always be accomplished alone. Make sure you find other people to help you on your child's language journey – it will be easier and more pleasant for all of you!

When does OPOL work best?

An OPOL approach works best when it is structured to allow for balance between the two languages of the home. This needs to take into account the language input from outside the home as well, which is often disregarded in the literature on OPOL. If the language of schooling is the same as one of the parental languages, that needs to be considered when planning for input in the other language. OPOL can also be used in situations where the parents speak different languages at home and a third language is used in the community/schooling. In this case, neither parental language is dominant due to outside support, so there is slightly less risk of the community language taking over completely. There is, however, a risk that one or both of the parental languages will end up in a situation where input is very limited. This is common when one or both parents work long hours and especially if a parent travels often. While there is no easy fix for these situations, it's important to remember the other aspects of the language plan that we can work with to increase input in a language. We will look at some strategies further on in this chapter. Worksheet 3 will help you map out the input for the languages in your Family Language Plan.

Minority language at home (MLaH)

A less written about but very often successful approach is the MLaH approach. The structure of this approach is that both parents use the minority language with the children when at home, and the other language is learned/used outside the home. This is generally through childcare and schooling, and reflects the situation of many/most immigrant families. The clear benefit of this approach is that the minority language plays a major part in the children's lives, so it is less likely to be swamped by the majority language. It also gives the family a clear framework for language use that is simple and attainable. Some families find that OPOL is difficult to work with because of the one-sided conversations between parents and children in each language. MLaH creates an environment in which the home language is shared by all and functions as the *family language*.

Issues with MLaH

One of the common challenges of MLaH is that the learning of the majority language is very much laissez-faire. Parents enrol their children in daycare in the majority language and depend on the sponge myth to ensure that their children will naturally and easily acquire the language. This can be successful but it is not a guarantee of acquisition. I have met many families over the years who made this choice, in the full expectation that their child would be fluent in the language in months. Sometimes the lack of success is down to over-optimism or clarity of expectations. For example, in the Netherlands many childcare workers are comfortable speaking English and/or other languages, so they might use English/another language with a non-Dutch speaking child, thinking that it will be helpful. Another factor is how well the child reacts to being dropped into an environment where they do not speak the language. Some children thrive but others isolate themselves and do not interact enough to gain language skills. These children are also often very unhappy, which is not an ideal condition for learning anything, language included. If childcare/daycare is a part of your Family Language Plan it needs to be clear to all involved what the expectations are, and the child's well-being needs to be attended to as well.

When MLaH extends into schooling, there are key areas that the parents need to be prepared to support, which we will look at in the section on school-based bilingualism.

Domains of use

The final approach we will look at is the domains of use approach. In many ways the most flexible approach, this is also one that needs clear planning and attention in order to work towards success. In a domains of use approach, language is considered not only as an attribute of a person, but as connected to time, place or topic. All participants use the same language within a domain, as far as they are able. It encourages all family members to participate in all languages, even if it is not 'their' language and even if they don't have native speaker competence. I've worked with many families over the years on a variety of domains of use based plans, and one thing that comes through strongly is their sense of languages being a family effort.

Domains of use can include some of these variations:

- By time:
  - family dinners in one language (or other specified time)
  - days of the week or alternating weeks
- By topic:
  - school discussions in school language
  - religion – language associated with church/mosque/synagogue or other
- By place
  - home/school
  - by room in the house
- By person
  - who is present
  - who is participating in the conversation

Families can determine for themselves what makes sense for their languages and their lives, and this makes the implementation less fraught with difficulty. If your family needs more Polish input and the only time you are all together is dinner time, then make sure that dinner time is high-quality Polish time. Domains of use also allows parents to use more than one language, and to share the responsibility for all languages in the Family Language Plan.

Benefits of domains of use

Although the planning and scheduling can sometimes feel daunting, there are both practical and affective benefits to a domains of use strategy. In the first instance, it provides a clear structure for providing more input in a minority language, which can be difficult in OPOL and MLaH approaches. In the second instance, domains of use is particularly powerful as it models both parents as bilinguals and both parents as supportive of both languages. It is also an answer to a frequent complaint that OPOL parents have: the lack of a 'family' language. In fact, families using this method can end up as very fluid, comfortable bilinguals who can switch between languages at ease. It can also encourage parents to become more fluent or comfortable in each other's languages, even if they never become fluent speakers – you don't need to be a native speaker or a 'perfect' speaker to use another language with your children. I have met many families that had quite competitive attitudes to the two parental languages, with each parent feeling their language was more important, or more neglected. A domains of use approach can introduce a more collaborative attitude and provide better linguistic and sociolinguistic support for each language.

Combining elements of different approaches

Raising bi/multilingual children is not always as straightforward as we expect it to be, and very often one set approach will not work for a family. The three approaches we have looked at are not mutually exclusive. You can take elements of each and integrate them into your Family Language Plan in ways that make sense for your family and have the best chance of achieving the desired results. You may decide to use OPOL when you are alone with the children, MLaH when you are all together, and elements of domains of use to support a second minority language. The bottom line for language acquisition is adequate input, no matter what approach you are using, so this should always be the key in Family Language Plan development.

Sequential Bilingualism: Learning Another Language at School

This section is based on the 'Parents as Language Partners' seminar which I have developed and delivered in schools all over the world. The purpose of the seminar, and this section, is to provide parents with a clear understanding of the situation of children who are learning through a second/additional language, and how parental support can be key to success.

Research stemming from Canadian immersion schools in the 1980s and showing positive effects from school-based bilingualism has had a profound impact on attitudes towards immersion/bilingual education. If asked, most people would now say that they think learning another language through schooling is a good thing and has positive results for children. While this certainly can be the case, it is more true for children who are experiencing what we call prestige or high-status bilingualism, which is considered to be additive bilingualism: the child keeps developing in their first/dominant language and adds another language to their repertoire. This type of bilingualism through education has been developed for majority language children learning another high-status language. Thus, in Canada, English-speaking children going to French immersion schools are in this privileged situation; they speak one high-status language (English) and are acquiring a second (French) through school. Research consistently indicates that children in this situation generally do not suffer any negative educational consequences either for their academic development or for their own-language development, and have the added benefits of becoming bilingual. From this perspective, bilingualism through education is a win-win situation for children.

There are significant differences in outcomes for children who are not in the high status–high status combination of languages, and unfortunately they are largely not as positive. Extensive research by UNESCO, UNICEF and researchers in a variety of countries has clearly shown that children who are minority language speakers going into majority language schools do not, globally, have positive language development outcomes or academic outcomes. The impact of being schooled in a language that you are learning is variable and is influenced by the child's individual profile, the family background and situation and how the school nurtures (or does not nurture) language learner students. The information in this section provides parents with the knowledge and practical strategies to support their children through the dual challenge of learning *language* and learning *content*, to achieve the best experience for the children and the best chance of success, linguistically and academically.

Elements for Success in School-based Bilingualism

While personal factors to do with individual children and families have influence on the process and outcomes of school-based bilingualism, there are three areas related to the school that have an impact on experiences and outcomes. The first is language status, and the relationship between the status of the home language(s) and that of the school and community language. The second is the school language policy and whether it is supportive of continuing bilingualism or not. The third is literacy: developing literacy in the home language guards against language loss.

Language status

One of the unfortunate realities of bilingualism is that success or failure is often determined by language status. Languages can be high status, low status or neutral. This is not an unchangeable rating – it depends on where you are and what other languages are involved. For example, in the Netherlands, Spanish is a high-status language. It is a popular choice in schools, and many people learn Spanish in order to travel to Spanish-speaking countries. In the United States in many places, Spanish is viewed as a low-status language because of its associations with undocumented immigrants and low-status workers. The same language is viewed completely differently because of the cultural and institutional factors connected with it in each environment. So how does language status affect bilingualism, and is there anything that can be done to counteract the effects?

The answer to the first question lies in sociocultural attitudes and government support. Language status is a complex phenomenon made up of people's attitudes towards the home country of the language, people's attitudes towards speakers of that language and institutional attitudes about the language. For example, all children in the Netherlands learn English at school. English is seen on mainstream television and many Dutch children will hear their parents using English at some point. All of these together give children the message that English is useful and desirable. This means that children who are native speakers of English are not (usually) pressured to give up their own language in favour of Dutch. While the school will often not actively encourage them to use English at school outside of English classes (although it does sometimes happen that even English is banned), it is generally viewed as positive to be able to speak English. However, children arriving at school with low-status languages face a different prospect. A Polish-speaking child will often/frequently have no support or encouragement institutionally to help them keep using Polish, and these languages are more likely to be banned or discouraged in covert ways. Because of this pattern, it's important for parents to consider the status of their language and plan to 'boost' it if they feel that it is considered a low-status language where they are living.

While my examples above are from the Netherlands, there are many other places where minority and/or low-status languages are either outright banned or strongly discouraged, stemming from the incorrect assumption that using any language other than the school language will interfere with learning. For this reason it is critical, whenever possible, to choose a school carefully – one that includes and celebrates other languages and cultures rather than one that demands assimilation. The bottom line is that language status is important in bilingualism, but informed and active parents can help promote the status of, and therefore the sustainability of, their language within their families and communities. Planning for this should be a part of your Family Language Plan. Worksheet 4 will help you with your school choice decision, if this is part of your Family Language Plan.

School language policy

The second factor that impacts success is language policy. All schools have a language policy, although it may not be a written document. Leadership and staff attitudes towards bilingualism and bi/multilingual children will influence how they view and deal with languages in the school. Most international schools will have a written language policy, but there is very often divergence between the written and lived language policy in a school. Broadly speaking, schools can have two types of policy approach. The first is an additive policy. This means they recognise and embrace the value of the language(s) the children arrive with, and are very clear about the process of adding a new language – the school language – to a child's linguistic repertoire. How it is expressed in the written policy (if they have one) may differ, but in practice it means that all the languages of the children are visible in the school in different ways, and that they are encouraged to use their languages for learning. In many schools they are encouraged to use their languages only informally, in play and at break times and with same-language peers. Increasingly in schools, there is a growing recognition of how important and useful children's home/dominant languages can be for promoting additional language learning, for academic learning, for promoting positive multilingual identities and for raising interest in language learning for monolingual students. This type of policy and practice, known as *additive bilingualism*, is most likely to result in successfully bi/multilingual students.

The second policy approach that schools can take is a *subtractive* one. This policy approach is arguably the most common globally, when we consider the numbers of children in multilingual countries that are not educated in their mother tongue/home languages, and whose languages have no place in their education. In a subtractive approach, the children are given the message that their language is not for school. Some schools do this overtly, by having rules that only the school language is allowed. Historically, and currently, there are many incidences of children being punished for using their own language at school. Even schools that do not have an outright ban on other languages, or that on the surface seem to be supportive of multilingualism, may in fact have a covert subtractive policy. This may be apparent in 'reasonable' rules about language use – for example, stipulating that children can use their own languages outside but not inside the classrooms. They may also discourage parents from speaking their own languages at the school, for a variety of seemingly positive reasons.

Language status often plays a large part in which languages are negatively viewed at school, with immigrant/minority languages being perceived as interfering with the acquisition of the majority language. In this way, the rules the schools make will often be presented as being in the best interests of the children, when this is contrary to what we know from research. This approach is called *subtractive bilingualism* – the plan is to subtract one language in favour of another. At best it is damaging to the children's first language(s), and at worst it is also damaging to their acquisition of the school language and to their academic progress.

Home language literacy

They also found that the main variable in students' achievement in English is whether or not they have kept up literacy in their mother tongue. (Carder, 2007: 99)

The third factor in success with school-based bilingualism is literacy. If bilingualism is the ability to use two or more languages, is literacy a necessary part of this? Do you need to be able to read and write a language in order to qualify as 'bilingual'? The answer to the first question – is literacy necessary for bilingualism – is 'not really'. People all over the world speak two or more languages, and are literate in only one, or even none. It is not necessary to be literate to be bilingual. However, literacy does make it easier to maintain a language, especially if you live outside a community of practice. Literacy brings you access to a host of ways to gather passive input (reading) and use a language (writing) which may not be available to you if you are not surrounded by speakers of this language. Reading is also one of the best ways to grow vocabulary in a language, so if a child has little daily exposure (in the form of oral input) to a language, being able to read will help them acquire a better vocabulary and therefore be able to use the language better. For parents raising bilingual children, literacy is always a good goal for at least two of their languages, and if there is one school language and one home language, literacy in both will provide opportunities to use either going forward in life.

Learning language; learning through language

> It is a universal yet not generally recognized truism that learning in a new language that is not one's own provides a double set of challenges: not only of learning a new language but also of learning new knowledge in that language. (UNESCO, 2007: iii)

If you have chosen, or are required, to put your children into a school where they will be learning the language of instruction, it is important to remember that they will be doing two jobs for the first years of schooling. I call this 'wearing two hats'. Their first hat is their 'language learner' hat. While wearing this hat they will be paying attention to the language around them, and their cognitive attention will be on deciphering and storing new language. Their second hat is their 'academic' hat. While wearing this hat they will be paying attention to the content that is being presented, investigated and learned. The two hats analogy is useful to contextualise their situation and recognise that there are very obviously consequences to the dual nature of their educational experiences. It is also important to appreciate that while young children can appear to pick up a new language quickly at school, in fact fully acquiring a language for academic purposes takes a long time, so they will be balancing those two hats for much longer than you might think.

Professor Jim Cummins, one of the most renowned researchers in the field, proposed a model for understanding school-based bilingual development which identifies two different types of language proficiency (Cummins, 2008). The first is basic interpersonal communicative skills (BICS). This is the language we use every day in social situations, and is not as cognitively challenging. In terms of schools, it is the language of routines, particularly common interactions between peers, and general, everyday interactions. It takes children from one to three years in full-time education to be functioning at the same level as a fluent speaker of the same age. This is often surprising to parents, who feel that their children have progressed or should progress more quickly, but it is the reality of how complex even BICS-level language can be.

The second type of proficiency is cognitive academic language proficiency (CALP). This is the kind of language we need to engage in challenging academic content: to evaluate, analyse, hypothesise and all the other deeper level thinking skills needed in education. It takes children from three to nine years of full-time education to acquire this type of language to the same level of functioning as a fluent speaker of the same age. During this period of three to nine years, a child who is both a language learner and a content learner is not able to attend to academic content in the same way as children who have already mastered the school language. During this time of wearing two hats there are four key areas of challenge to be aware of and to consider as crucial to development. We will look at each of these and identify key strategies that parents can use in order to properly support children in becoming successful both linguistically and academically.

Issues for learning

(I)   Cognitive development
(II)   Literacy
(III) Content learning
(IV)   Confidence and socialisation

I. Cognitive development

> The level of development of children's mother tongue is a strong predictor of their second language development. (Cummins, 2001: 3)

How much attention you need to pay to the issue of continued cognitive development depends on the age of the child when starting school in a new language. Generally speaking, the younger the child the more attention is needed. The reasons are related to the relationship between the language we think with and how we develop our thinking processes. What we know from research is that there is a strong connection between the strength of a child's home/first/dominant language and how well and how quickly they acquire a new language at school. Basically, the stronger children are in their own language(s), the better they will be able to learn a new language at school.

I illustrate the relationship between language development and cognitive development in my parent seminars using the illustration in Figure 2.2.

When babies are born, they immediately start climbing up the hill of cognitive development. There are different stages of cognitive development and they have different names depending on the school of thought, but there is general agreement about the trajectory of cognitive development, which moves from concrete (logical) to abstract thought at around 11–12 years of age.

Imagine a child living with Korean-speaking parents, living in the United States. The child climbs the first four years of their hill in Korean, so that when they are four years old they can do all the things that a four-year-old can do with their brain – they can think like a four-year-old, reason like a four-year-old, express themselves like a four-year-old, all through the Korean language. When they are four, their parents put them into an English-language school. The school advises (as many schools sadly do) the parents to start speaking English at home, to help their child learn English more quickly. The parents take this advice and drop Korean in favour of English. The child is obviously not capable of accessing the same kind of thinking in English as in Korean, as they hardly know any English. Consequently, cognitive development becomes more difficult, because

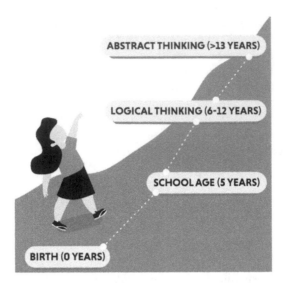

Figure 2.2 The hill of cognitive development

everyone is talking to them in a language they don't understand. A year later, at five years old, this child can still not think, reason, talk like a five-year-old in English (remember it takes three to nine years to catch up). But if nobody has been talking to them in Korean, and helping them develop both their thinking skills and their language to go along with these, they are likely not functioning as a five-year-old should in Korean either. This is a situation where the lack of appropriate, age-level input in a language that the child can use effectively can have detrimental effects on their overall development.

Now imagine that the school gave better advice, or that the parents ignored the school's flawed (but frequently given) advice, and they kept talking to their child in Korean, including about what happens at school every day. A year later, when the child is five years old, they are still not functioning at a five-year-old level in English. But they are functioning at a five-year-old level in Korean, and a five-year-old brain can learn more effectively than a four-year-old brain, so the child is now a stronger learner of English because of the strength of their development in Korean. Their continued cognitive development through their own language improves their ability to learn the school language (English). The home language is the language that you have to rely on for a child's development until that three to nine year period for developing CALP is finished and they are fully cognitively mature and academically at a native speaker level in the school language. This is why there is a strong link between level of the home language and level of the school language. It is not coincidental; it is that one drives the other, and the strength of the home language will pull the school language up the hill with it.

The reason why schools still give the advice to stop using the home language and start using English is that it sounds logical: 'Your child's English isn't good enough. Start using it at home because more English will make their English better.' But in fact it backfires and often children end up without a fully developed language for cognitive and academic purposes. Another analogy I use with parents is that it's a bit like a game of Jenga. If you try to pull the bottom block out from a tower of Jenga blocks, it's very hard to do so without toppling the whole tower. And even if you manage to get the bottom block out without toppling the tower, the tower becomes unstable and is not as solid as it should be. The bottom block is the child's dominant language(s) from birth; it is the basis on which other languages can be successfully built.

Parental strategies for supporting cognitive development

How much you need to do at home to support continued cognitive development depends on how old your child is when they start school in another language; the younger the child, the more attention needs to be paid to this. The following strategies can be used as a part of your Family Language Plan for supporting home language(s) growth:

(a) *Continue to use your own language with your child*, even if given advice to the contrary. The school's job is the school language; your job is your language.
(b) *Be aware of the need for language to keep developing.* Make sure you are paying attention to extending vocabulary and expression and not using only basic language.
(c) *Talk about school topics*, to make sure that their ability in the home language keeps pace with the types of things they are learning about in school.
(d) *Make sure you are engaging in cognitively challenging activities in your language*: playing games, reading stories, telling jokes. All of these will help your child's cognitive development to continue despite not being at school in their own language.

II. Literacy

(They) also found that the main variable in students' achievement *in English* is whether or not they have kept up literacy in their mother tongue. (Carder, 2007: 99)

Research on language learner students in English language only or bilingual schools clearly demonstrates the benefits of maintaining and developing the home language. This is associated with continued cognitive development, but is a strong argument for aiming to achieve literacy in the home language as well, especially when the school literacy is in a non-dominant language. This finding is supported in other contexts too, with children of immigrant parents in various countries performing better educationally when they have strong levels of literacy in their own languages.

Learning to read in a language in which you do not understand is challenging at any age, in different ways. In this section we will look at the challenges for children who are learning to read and write for the first time, and for older children who can already read and write in another language.

Primary literacy in a new school language

Learning to read is something that can be exciting and enjoyable, or difficult and disheartening. For many children it is a mixture, but if we want our children to grow up with a love of reading, we need to ensure that it is more the former than the latter. When young children have their first literacy experiences in a language that they are learning it is unfortunately more likely to be difficult than enjoyable, unless both the school and parents work together on providing the best support. For children who start school one to two years before literacy becomes a focus, the opportunity to learn some of the school language before literacy is immensely beneficial. Unfortunately, many schools these days start literacy at a very young age, and do not allow children this space for language development. It used to be traditional that formal literacy instruction began in the year children were six to seven years old, and this is aligned with what we know about cognitive development. There are countries that have maintained the age of literacy at six to seven years (the Netherlands, Finland, Sweden, etc.), but most schools now, and certainly most international schools, begin literacy much earlier, some as early as four years old. Children who are both language learners and beginning readers at the same time need substantial support, and a recognition that their journey will not parallel that of the students who already speak the school language.

Parental strategies for supporting primary literacy

Reading in a new language: How can you help?

(1) *Understand how reading works.* One of the key things you can do to support your child is to talk to them about literacy in your own language. Discussions about what reading is and how we do it will help young children who haven't yet processed the potential of the written word.
(2) *Literacy strategies.* Model different literacy strategies when you read to them, such as how to find the boundaries of words and what letters look like in lower and upper case. Helping them learn to tune into illustrations as cues to understanding content will also help them when they begin reading.
(3) *Content before decoding.* One phenomenon I encounter frequently with children who are learning to read before mastering the language is that they attach too much importance to decoding – to being able to 'sound out' the words in the right way. Often, they are hyper-focused on this, because decoding is a main focus in many schools. At home, make sure to emphasise understanding the story before decoding. When they bring a reading book home, talk it through in your own language before even looking at the English words, so that they can attach the words they are sounding out to the story they already understand. This is key to helping them develop a love of reading rather than a skill in decoding.

Secondary literacy in a new school language

Children who start school in a new language after already having had some of their education in their own language have an advantage in skills but a disadvantage in terms of expectations. In the first instance, they have had the experience of becoming literate in their own language as their primary literacy, which we know to be beneficial. It is also the case that strong literacy in the first/home language is linked to better results in a acquiring a second language through schooling. Again, building on a strong base and a stronger cognitive foundation means that the home language is less likely to suffer or to be lost, especially if parents make the effort to maintain home language literacy practices outside school. On the other hand, the literacy needs of older children are more significant. We generally consider that children spend the first two to three years *learning to read*, and then they move towards *reading to learn*. At this point, much more of the curricular knowledge is transmitted through reading and writing, and not being able to read and write to the appropriate level has considerable effects on learning and on assessment.

Parental strategies for supporting secondary literacy

Learning to read again: How can you help?

(1) *Patience and encouragement.* The most important thing parents can do is to be understanding. It's difficult becoming less competent than you were at school, and children don't need extra pressure. It will take time to bring the new literacy up to the necessary level, and there is no set time frame. Children will vary as individuals, but also the distance between the language they are already literate in and the new language will impact how long it will take (for example, learning a new writing system will take longer).

(2) *Try to find familiar books in the school language.* If they have already read a story or know a lot about the topic from reading about it in their own language, the school language version will be more accessible.

(3) *Make sure they keep reading in their own language, for pleasure.* While they are learning to read in the school language it won't be fun, and it's important that they still engage in reading just for the pleasure of reading.

Reading: Who does what, and why?

One of the questions that comes up in almost every seminar I do is related to reading. Most of the families I work with are lucky enough to have children's books available in both family languages. Children (being often contrary) tend to pick up a book from the 'other' language and refuse any attempt to be directed to a book in the 'right' language for the reading parent. So what is a parent to do? Stumble through in an attempt to read the Dutch book? Refuse altogether? Or, the third and preferred option, read the book in the 'right' language? I think that parents should never refuse to read a book their child has chosen. For parents who are passing on a minority language, consistency of language input is important. So the parent becomes translator for the moment, and reads the book in their preferred language. This is easy enough when the book is a baby book, with words alone or simple text. But what about when the books get harder? And the parent doesn't actually understand? Well, at this point, the parent becomes author ... and creates their own story to go with the pictures, engaging their child about the content along the way.

Now wouldn't it just be easier to say, 'Sorry, honey. That book is in Daddy's language, so you have to wait for Daddy to read it'? Yes, of course. But the message you want to send to your child is that reading, in all their languages, is worth the effort. For a child to experience the same story, told in different languages and sometimes even in different ways, is a demonstration of the dynamic nature of both bilingualism and reading, and that, in my opinion, is worth the effort.

Home language literacy

Although we often consider simultaneous bilingualism to be better than sequential bilingualism, there is no evidence that simultaneous biliteracy (learning to read in two or more languages at the same time) is better than sequential biliteracy. Children can and do learn to read in the second (or subsequent) language any time from months to years after learning to read and write in the first language. There are no demonstrated negative effects to learning to read first in one language and then in the next. This means that there is no need to pressure or overload a child to achieve literacy in both languages early on in schooling. In my opinion, if there are no clear benefits to simultaneous biliteracy, then it is (generally) better to wait until the child is comfortably literate in the school language before formally beginning literacy training in the second language. For this reason, I usually advise parents who have children becoming literate in the school language to wait until their children are confident readers before introducing literacy in the home language. If children are expressing an interest in literacy in the home language, parents can absolutely follow their lead, but without putting any pressure on accuracy, spelling, etc.

Once a child has gained literacy skills in one language – presuming the alphabets are the same – literacy in the other language comes quite easily. Even if alphabets/writing systems are different, a lot of the basics of literacy are the same, so the second can still build on the first. What you can do to set them up for success is to continue to read at home every day with them in your own language, especially on similar topics to those that they're reading about at school. Building their language skills in their own language will create a strong base for when they are ready to learn to read and write. If the home language(s) share an alphabet with the school language you can encourage them to experiment with writing. Surprising as it may seem, children who speak alphabetic languages can write before they can read. In order to read you have to understand the phonetic system of a language completely to decode it accurately; writing is an entirely creative endeavour – you write down how you think it ought to look. Encourage them to engage in writing as a creative process; it reinforces for them that this is a language that they will use one day in the written form as well. It's important not to correct their early efforts, as then it becomes something that is pressurised and they may back away from it.

Parental strategies for supporting home language literacy

(1) *Prioritise literacy in the school language first.*
(2) *Engage in literacy-type activities in the other language(s)* – reading out loud, alphabet/writing system play, writing play – every day.

(3) *Have a plan for how you will help your child to become literate in the other language.*
(4) *Remember that reading and writing should be fun for children* – they need to learn in a positive way, when they are cognitively ready.

Community language schools

Many parents take advantage of the existence of community language schools (usually on Saturdays or Sundays) to support a minority language. These bring together families from the same background, with the goal of teaching literacy in the minority language. This provides support in terms of a community with a shared language, and an outside source of language expertise.

While this is a very good plan in theory, the reality is that many of these schools use an old-fashioned pedagogy which does not inspire the students to want to learn the language but instead inspires resentment for having to be in school at the weekend. Although these weekend classes can be invaluable, especially for literacy in languages with different writing conventions, parents often need to work with the school to provide programming that is motivational and that supports positive attitudes. Some community language schools offer subjects in a language, rather than just formal language teaching. Many connect language to culture, and have celebrations and develop knowledge of heritage. Other are linked to the practice of religion, where the language is central to a community's religious practices. All of these can be promoted positively, if the environment is encouraging and supportive and not pressurised and punitive. If a community language school is a part of your Family Language Plan, don't be afraid to get involved and help make it successful.

III. Content learning

The most valuable learning tool children have is the language they already know. (Lightbown, in Chalmers, 2019: 8)

Another important parental job is to support content learning at home. Thinking back to the analogy of children wearing two hats, a language learning hat and an academic hat, it follows that keeping up with content learning will be a challenge. We can also connect this to the window of time (three to nine years) it takes children to achieve age-appropriate cognitive and linguistic proficiency in a new school language; during this window they will not be accessing content in the same ways as fluent speakers. Having a clear plan to support content learning at home will help your children arrive at school with prior knowledge that they can scaffold language onto. If they are sitting in class and they don't know anything about the topic and they don't know the language, it's very hard for them to develop either content understanding or language. Connect with your children's teachers to find out what topics they are working on and have dinner table discussions about these, or have your children do some research on the topics in their home language(s). How much children can do independently will depend on their age and literacy skills in their own language, but by going to school with some understanding of the concepts they will have better access to the language being used. This also supports continued development in the home language(s): as they learn about new things through the language, that language will grow too, so it is beneficial for both school access and home language maintenance.

In the three to nine year window that it will take children to become proficient, parents also need to moderate their expectations about how their children will do in school. Certain aspects of children's learning will be affected in this time frame primarily by the fact that part of their cognitive time and attention is devoted to language and not solely to content.

Parental strategies for supporting content learning

(1) *Use home language resources.* With children who are literate in their own language, finding resources about key topics in that language will support understanding and vocabulary development.
(2) *Home language conversations.* With younger learners, simply have conversations about the things they are learning about in school, and find out from the teacher what is important.
(3) *Homework.* Continue doing homework as much as possible in the home language. While the maths book may be in English, if they didn't understand the English explanation it will be more effective to discuss the maths in their stronger language, to ensure comprehension.
(4) *Support writing through the home language.* For older learners, writing an outline of a writing task in the home language can provide them with space to think first about their ideas, and then think about how to write it in the school language.

Translanguaging for learning

Translanguaging is the process of making meaning, shaping experiences, gaining understanding and knowledge through the use of two languages. (Baker, 2011: 288)

Translanguaging, at home and at school, is a new framework for understanding how languages can work together to support development. First identified in Welsh-language schools in Wales, and since extended as a theory and a pedagogy around the world, there are now many different practices associated with the term. In this discussion we will look only at a practical aspect for supporting learning in a second language.

There used to be much made of the need to keep languages separate so that people don't mix them or get confused, but research is showing that actually languages are complementary and not in competition. In terms of supporting children learning a new language at school, this means that we can and should use children's languages together to build meaning rather than trying to isolate them. This is true both for literacy and for content support. Parents can use their own language at home with their child to help them learn to read in the school language as mentioned above, to make sure that they understand the story and that they understand the concepts in the story. From this, move on to helping them decode the words in the school language and connect them to the concepts you have already talked about in your language. Many of the strategies mentioned in the section on supporting content rely on translanguaging as well – building knowledge in one language and transferring it to the other. More schools are starting to investigate and implement translanguaging, especially in the international sector, so you may hear your school talking about it and encouraging students to use their own languages at school as well, to help support understanding of content and language development from the stronger language to the language being learned.

IV. Confidence and socialisation

> The language we use reflects who we are, where we come from, and the shared histories we have as members of our communities. (Chalmers, 2019: 21)

The final area of challenge for language learners in schools is confidence and socialisation. This area is often neglected or not even considered, as an effect of the 'children are sponges' myth. The majority of children experience some negative impact on their confidence and ability to socialise when they are put into a school where they cannot use their own language any more. Much like adults thrust into the same situation, they may feel nervous, intimidated or isolated. How strong the impact is depends on a wide variety of factors, such as their age, their personality, the school attitude and the availability of peers who speak their language. Very young children will not process the experience in the same way as older children, but may be perturbed because they don't understand *why* they don't understand, or why others don't understand them. Older learners may feel disenfranchised – they go from being fully functional learners in one environment to being outsiders who cannot speak or learn in the ways they are used to doing.

To help parents (and teachers!) understand what this feels like, in my seminars I make them take part in an activity in which they have to talk for one minute about what they do, without using any words that have the letter 'n' in them (or another letter/sound of a similar frequency in their own language). If you take a minute to do this, you will feel for that minute what language learners in school feel like: you have to think very hard for every word, and you often have to choose words that aren't quite right and that sound a bit strange. This illustrates the sudden loss of competence that language learners feel when the language available to them is suddenly less than that which they are used to, and the language that they do have makes them sound less intelligent or knowledgeable than they really are. Parents' final job is to make sure that they are providing emotional support and paying attention to building/maintaining self-confidence during this phase.

Parental strategies for supporting confidence and socialisation

(1) *Continued use of the home language as a key element of identity and culture.* The more confident children feel in themselves, the more likely they will be to adapt and socialise in the new school and seek out interaction and therefore become more confident and become better speakers.

(2) *Ensuring children experience 'competence' at home*, both as language users and as language learners.
(3) *Make efforts to have the school develop positive pedagogy involving other languages*, so that all children can be seen as experts in the school, and competent in *language*, if not in the school language yet.

Making the Right School Choice for your Family Language Plan

One of the most important elements, apart from the parental languages, in a Family Language Plan is the choice of school. Of course, not every family has the ability to control this element of their language plan, but if you do have a choice, it's important to choose wisely.

There are three elements to look at when choosing a school:

(1) Language
(2) Culture
(3) Personality (of your child, and the school)

The first element to consider is language. If you are a bilingual family, with one majority language and one minority language, it's best to try and balance the input by using school to bolster a minority language, if at all possible. If you are a monolingual family introducing an outside language (such as Dutch, in the Netherlands), then school is the logical place to do it. Basically, if you have the possibility of using school choice to balance the languages in your child's environment, and to help them achieve literacy goals in two or more languages, then this is a good thing to do.

However, there is also the aspect of culture to be considered. If you are living in a place where you are not 'local' but you need or want your children to fit in, linguistically and culturally, a local language school would be a better choice. I worked with a lot of families who were in the Netherlands indefinitely, and they struggled with the choice of international schooling versus Dutch schooling. Realistically, if you are going to be living somewhere for a long time, you will want your children to be able to participate in local culture and this is the best way to help this happen. Similarly, if a child has one Dutch parent and one 'other', you need to carefully consider the linguistic benefits of international schooling versus the cultural benefits of a local school.

Finally, when all the above feels unclear and unhelpful, you need to consider your child's personality and the schools that are available. I believe that finding a school that 'fits' your child is more important than any linguistic or cultural agenda the parents may have. How your child feels at school, how they fit in and how they perform academically are factors that will help influence the rest of their academic careers. Finding a school where they feel at home and can truly learn to love learning will benefit them immensely, and putting your child in the 'wrong' school can do a lot of damage. It's also important to remember that the 'right' school may not be the same for all the children in one family (unfortunately). Yes, language goals are important, but you can adjust your plan around the school language and find support and success from other avenues. Yes, cultural integration is important, but not at the expense of a child's spirit.

Summer language loss: What can we do?

While children are usually delighted to start the summer holidays, educators are often concerned about the learning that children may lose over the holidays. In the case of children who go to school in a language not spoken around them (in the home or community) there is another serious side-effect of the summer break: *summer language loss.* Here are some ideas to help parents lessen the summer language loss for their children:

(1) *Enforce good reading habits.* Children should read every day in the summer, in the school language and in their own language as well. It's best if the children choose what to read themselves, but a good librarian can help them make choices that are age/level appropriate and that will meet their interests. Look for a summer reading programme at the local library or online if your child needs competition to get them reading!

(2) *Read to your children.* Parents need good reading habits too! Read to your children in your own language, and in the school language if you are comfortable with that. Have conversations around what you are reading, in any language.

(3) *Use screen time strategically.* If your child loves cartoons, find some in the school language for them to watch. If they are movie fans, get movies in the school language, watch them with subtitles and compare what people are saying! This helps focus in on language use and keeps them thinking in the school language.

(4) *Plan for school language conversation time.* If parents are comfortable using the school language (you don't need to be perfect, and accent doesn't matter!), consider planning a block of time several times a week to do an activity together in the school language. This could be playing a game, having a conversation or any other shared activity. By making it a planned activity, you can be sure that the school language won't take over from the home language, but you still give your children some time to use the language regularly.

For some families, the summer is the time when they go back to their home country and focus on building their children's language skills in this important language. This is also very valuable and shouldn't be sacrificed. What you are looking for is balance, between the needs of home language development over the summer and lessening the summer language loss effect.

Updating and Evolving Your Plan

When the mother tongue becomes a minority language: One family's story

This story is that of a family who contacted me with concerns about their situation. I am sharing it here as I think it illustrates several different issues parents face when trying to implement a Family Language Plan.

The family are from a country in the Middle East, and have Arabic and English as the two languages in their language plan. They began their family in the Middle East and chose the OPOL approach, with the mother speaking in Arabic and the father in English (he is also a fluent Arabic speaker). After a move to the United States, the children now have much more exposure to English than Arabic. The family will move back to the Middle East in a few years' time.

So, the question being posed is: 'When should you change your Family Language Plan, and how should it be done?'.

A Family Language Plan is a dynamic document, not one written in stone. We make a plan based on our language goals for our children, and the best means to reach those goals in our present situation. The OPOL method is ideal for families who want to transmit two languages to their children and have the possibility of having one parent using each language. However, in some cases it is quite clear which is the priority language. For this family, the priority language is Arabic – the language of both parents and their greater community and culture. English is a great addition to their children's languages, but the priority must remain with the home language.

Because the family is now living in an English-dominant environment, it is important to balance the input of the two languages as much as possible, which means increasing the amount of Arabic spoken. There are two ways to do this. The first is to adopt an MLaH approach. Using this method, both parents will speak to the children in Arabic at home and in English outside the home, leading to clear divisions between the two languages. This method is beneficial because it allows the children to hear more Arabic but still to use the community language outside the house (English). A stricter variation is that the parents speak Arabic all the time to the children, inside and outside the house, and the children learn English from the community (playschool, preschool and then school).

Which path to take depends very much on the parents. My preference would be for the children to hear as much Arabic as possible and not to feel that Arabic is something they can only use 'in private'. However, I am aware that using other languages in public, especially languages linked by some to negative stereotypes, can be uncomfortable in some situations. It's a terrible world we live in where people are judged by their home languages, but it would be disingenuous of me to pretend that this type of prejudice doesn't exist. So, each family needs to decide what language use they are comfortable with in the community in which they live.

Once the decision has been made for a change of plan, the next question is *how* to change. In this case, it's quite a simple transition for Dad to start speaking in Arabic with the children as well. There needs to be a family language discussion; even young children should be a part of the discussion when the language use changes – even a simple 'Daddy is going to start speaking to you the same way Mummy does' is a good beginning with a young child. Slightly older children can be given a more complete explanation about language: 'Because we want you to be able to use both your languages very well, and so we need to use more X language to help you with that.'

It is also beneficial to seek out other speakers of the minority language – parents and children – to help reinforce the message that the minority language isn't only for home.

This is particularly important when living in an English-speaking culture with English as the second language, as the pull towards 'English-only' is strong for young children.

By ensuring a better balance of input in the two languages, the children should grow in both languages and be able to reintegrate into Arabic-speaking life when the family returns to their home country. And once again, when the language situation has changed, the family can change their plan and go back to the OPOL method with the mother continuing in Arabic and the father returning to using English. The children will be old enough at the time of this transition to understand clearly the change in language use and the reasons for it, and will probably be keen to keep up their English, so it will hopefully be a smooth and easy transition.

When your life changes in any way that impacts the language situation in your family, you need to look at how those changes will impact your Family Language Plan and decide if it needs changing or updating. This can be anything from a house move, to a change in the people living in the home (addition of a family member or a family member moving out) or a change in school circumstances. In each of these cases, you must sit as a parent team and review the language goals you have set, checking if they are still appropriate and achievable in your new situation. Very often you will need to look at input, as changing circumstances often mean a shift in the balance of input for one or more languages.

You may also need to review and revise your plan simply because it isn't working. As I've said before, each child in your family will be unique in their language aptitudes, attitudes and motivation, so a plan that worked perfectly for one child may not work as well for a second child. Again, you may need to revise your goals to fit the new reality, or you may want to keep your goals but revise your plan to support them, to give better support where needed. Bi/multilingual families may have this discussion many times over the years, as raising bi/multilingual children is anything but predictable.

A stage at which many parents find the need to adapt their plan is when their children reach their teenage years. Young children can be fairly tolerant of the requirements of living as a multilingual, but as they get older, social pressures often come into play which cause older children/teens to start pulling away from one of their languages (usually the home language if it is different from the school/community language). At this point, the Family Language Plan needs to become a collaborative exercise, with the reluctant teens being given some flexibility, and some responsibility, for their own bilingual development. This may mean finding certain social resources in the home language, connecting with groups that have similar interests or investing more holiday time in a location where the language is spoken. It may also mean taking a step back and letting our teenagers have some space. If they are very reluctant, or even obstructive, it won't do any good to force them, and may even be damaging to their motivation and to family relationships. A compromise may be the parent continuing to speak the minority language at home, but not forcing the teenager to use it, and agreeing to use the majority language (if possible) outside the home. At this point it's important to look at the long-term objectives rather than trying to force the issue in the short term. A parent who is willing to talk, and be flexible, will be a better role model for positive bilingualism.

The Importance of Monolingual Situations for Bilingualism

I know, it sounds like a contradiction, but how is monolingualism important for bilingualism? One of the most pressing concerns that many bilingual or multilingual families face is how to get the children to use the minority language. Many parents I work with report that their child 'understands everything I say in Spanish (or Italian, or Polish or whichever language is the least used), but they never speak to me in Spanish!'. This is especially true of younger siblings and school-aged children. And this is where monolingual situations are important.

If you are the minority language parent, and you also speak/understand the majority language (and even sometimes if you don't), chances are that you have had or will have this problem at some point. Children can be thrifty with their linguistic energies and prefer to use the language that works with the most people. Personally, I'm not in favour of pretending not to understand when my children speak to me in a different language from the one I want (but I know of people who use this tactic successfully). If you don't want to say 'I don't understand' to get them to use the minority language, how can you encourage your children to actually use it?

'Monolingual situations' – this is what your children need. This means that they need to spend time with people who only speak the minority language (these people can pretend not to speak the majority language!). Your children need activities that only happen in the minority language. They need to be put in situations where they have no choice, if they want to communicate, but to use the minority language.

But how do you set about finding these elusive minority language situations? The easiest way is to find other speakers of your language, and have 'language playdates' where everyone understands that the priority is to encourage the children to see the usefulness of the language and experience a communicative need that cannot be satisfied without using the minority language. This requires some discipline on the part of the parents, to ensure that they don't 'slip' into the majority language, and it may take some time for the children to adapt to the linguistic tone of the group.

Another technique that has been found successful for families with young children is to introduce (in the home) 'monolingual' resources. For example, a game that was bought in France must be played in French, no? (*non?*), or a puzzle bought in Poland must be puzzled in Polish. If you set up this dynamic in your home when your children are young it can be a useful technique for several years, eventually being replaced by monolingual books (and DVDs and computer games). As children get older, you need to find their personal currency: what do they want to do strongly enough that they will do it in the minority language if that is their only choice? For one family I worked with, this was a Pokémon card trading club; if the child wanted to belong to the club and trade cards, he had to do it in French (the minority language). Some careful thinking and planning are required, but the pay-off in terms of linguistic progress for the children can be great, and definitely worth it.

Finally, the best monolingual situation of all is, of course, time spent in a place where the minority language is the majority language. Many families I work with spend all their holidays in the home country of the minority language parent; some families have two minority language parents and need to split their time between two places. For some families, however, travel to the 'home country' is not an option. So then, you try to bring your home country to you. A healthy Skype relationship with family and friends can be helpful, but be aware that it may take your children some time to adapt to this form of communication. Telephone is harder for children, but if it is your only option, spend some time developing their 'phone skills'. And of course you can always fall back on television – it isn't designed to be interactive, but if the parent sits with the child and asks questions and discusses what is happening (dialogic listening), then you can use this as a language development tool with older children.

It's not always an easy task setting up monolingual situations in a multilingual life, but the rewards in terms of language development are worth it, and integrating monolingual situations should be a part of any Family Language Plan.

Dropping a Language: Is It Ever the Right Choice?

> A loss of the minority language may have social, emotional, cognitive, and educational consequences for the child. (Baker & Wright, 2017: 120)

People often presume that if a bilingual child is struggling, the best thing to do is to 'drop' a language. I've worked with parents who have been given this advice by doctors, teachers, speech therapists, family and so on. It sounds fairly logical – if your child is struggling with two (or more) languages, just drop one and they will get better. But is it actually true?

The bottom line is that it is *not true* that dropping one language will help the other become stronger. Children who are getting adequate language input and who are struggling with bilingual language acquisition would also be struggling if they were learning only one language. And generally, children who are being raised bilingually have a true need for both languages, so it would do them no favours to drop one language. In addition, it isn't always obvious which language would be the best candidate for 'dropping'. A child who has heard two languages consistently and in amounts that are substantial may not be obviously dominant in one language or another, or they may have mixed dominance. If the choice is made to drop a language and the wrong one is chosen, the consequences can be severe and long lasting. With young children, parents often cannot really tell which language they are most mature in, in terms of cognitive development. If the strongest language by way of cognitive development is removed, you are left with a child who is at a cognitive disadvantage, and that can be hard to recover from and can have permanent effects on their learning.

I had the opportunity several years ago to present with Dr Annick De Houwer, who studies early bilingual acquisition, and she used an excellent analogy. Imagine your child is learning to play the guitar and the piano. They are better at the guitar, although you'd like them to be better at the piano. Will having them stop playing the guitar improve their piano playing? The answer is, of course, absolutely not. Only more practice or better teaching will improve your child's piano skills. In addition, the skills learned from playing the guitar (such as reading music) are useful to apply to learning the piano as well, so they are complementary rather than in competition. I think this illustrates very well the lack of relationship between dropping one language and improving the other. If your child is struggling, you need to consider giving them better input to learn from, or looking for outside resources (professional help, etc.) which will improve their language skills, not find a solution that may cause more problems (see the section in Chapter 3, 'Know When to Get Help', for more on this topic).

There is one situation in which I feel that dropping a language could be the right thing to do, and that is in cases where one language has been artificially introduced. For example, parents who decide to put their children in preschool or school in a new language may sometimes discover that their child has a language or learning difficulty. If the second language is obviously (from the age of introduction) not dominant, and the language is not necessary but was chosen for enrichment purposes, then there may be an argument for letting the second language go, simply because if the language isn't an important part of a child's environment, their success in acquiring it is likely to be limited anyway.

Summary: The Family Language Plan

In this section we have looked at a wide range of topics related to developing your Family Language Plan, from different approaches you can take, to how you support your children in different situations. Here are some of the key points we have looked at:

- A Family Language Plan is a longitudinal and adaptable plan which follows a child from birth (or later) through to the end of secondary school, in order to give the parents and child the best chance for success.
- The elements of family language planning are:
  ○ goal setting;
  ○ mapping out where the input in each language will come from (in terms of people and time);
  ○ deciding how literacy will be approached in each language; and
  ○ thinking about how challenges will be dealt with.
- A Family Language Plan is never written in stone, but is a guideline and a road map which is flexible if necessary.
- Explore approaches such as: one-parent, one-language; minority language at home; and domains of use. Look at the benefits and challenges and then decide if one or a combination of the approaches will suit your goals and family situation.
- School-based bilingualism creates the dual challenge of learning *language* and learning *content*.
- There are three elements for success in school-based bilingualism:
  ○ language status, particularly the relationship between the status of the home language(s) and that of the school and community language;

- ○ school language policy, whether written or unwritten, will affect your child/ren's success; and
  - ○ literacy makes it easier to retain a language through both passive (reading) and active (speaking) input.
- Basic interpersonal communicative skills (BICS) take one to three years to develop in a school setting.
- Cognitive academic language proficiency (CALP) takes three to nine years to acquire, with full-time education.
- Four types of challenges to watch for:
  - ○ cognitive development – age-appropriate learning in their home language will help child/ren manage both language learning and academic learning;
  - ○ literacy – pay attention to the timing of literacy, and focus on reading together;
  - ○ content learning – help your child/ren by providing content learning in their home language to supplement their learning at school; and
  - ○ confidence and socialisation – child/ren often experience some negative impact, so it is important for parents to provide emotional support and build confidence in the home language.

Further Resources

The following sources can provide valuable additional information and support about raising bi/multilingual children.

Francois Grosjean, PhD

All of Grosjean's articles available on *Psychology Today* are excellent. He is also the author of the book, *Bilingual: Life and Reality* (Harvard University Press, 2010). See https://www.psychologytoday.com/gb/blog/life-bilingual

Bilingualism Matters

Founded by Antonella Sorace and based at the University of Edinburgh, Bilingualism Matters is a research-based organisation that works with community groups to provide support to families raising bi/multilingual children. It now has 25 international branches in additional to its valuable website. See https://www.bilingualism-matters.ppls.ed.ac.uk/.

Books

For monolingual families who want to raise bilingual children

Jernigan, C. (2015) *Family Language Learning: Learn Another Language, Raise Bilingual Children*. Bristol: Multilingual Matters.

King, K. and Mackey, A. (2007) *The Bilingual Edge: Why, When and How to Teach Your Child a Second Language*. New York: Harper Collins.

For specific circumstances

Barron-Hauwaert, S. (2004) *Language Strategies for Bilingual Families: The One-Parent-One-Language Approach*. Clevedon: Multilingual Matters.

Barron-Hauwaert, S. (2011) *Bilingual Siblings: Language Use in Families*. Bristol: Multilingual Matters.

Braun, A. and Cline, T. (2014) *Language Strategies for Trilingual Families: Parents' Perspectives*. Bristol: Multilingual Matters.

Wang, X.-L. (2011) *Learning to Read and Write in the Multilingual Family*. Bristol: Multilingual Matters.

General

Harding-Esch, E. and Riley, P. (2003) *The Bilingual Family: A Handbook for Parents*. Cambridge: Cambridge University Press.

Meisel, J.M. (2019) *Bilingual Children: A Guide for Parents*. Cambridge: Cambridge University Press.

Pearson, B.Z. (2008) *Raising a Bilingual Child: A Step-by-Step Guide for Parents*. New York: Living Language.

Steiner, N. with Hayes, S.L. (2009) *7 Steps to Raising a Bilingual Child*. New York: AMACOM.

Reference

Baker, C. (2014) *A Parents' and Teachers' Guide to Bilingualism* (4th edn). Bristol: Multilingual Matters.

This is the one book that I recommend all families purchase. It is the most complete guide to all of the questions you can and will meet along your journey. Because it is in a Q&A format, you can look up a specific question and get a complete but manageable answer.

Academic (for parents who want to read more deeply on the underlying theories and research)

Costa, A. (2019) *The Bilingual Brain: And What It Tells Us about the Science of Language*. New York: Penguin Random House.

De Houwer, A. (2009) *An Introduction to Bilingual Development*. Bristol: Multilingual Matters.

Lightbown, P.M. and Spada, N. (2013) *How Languages are Learned* (4th edn). Oxford: Oxford University Press.

N.B. There are many, many more books available on the theme of raising bilingual/multilingual children. I recommend the above books as I have read them all and found them to be accurate (research-based), well-written and accessible.

Worksheet 4: Family Language Planning Template

This worksheet is where you move from articulating your goals to planning how you will help your child(ren) achieve those goals. Make a plan for each child.

Language 1:	Language 2:
Early years input:	*Early years input:*
School years input:	*School years input:*
Literacy plan:	*Literacy plan:*
Special issues:	*Special issues:*
Language 3:	**Language 4:**
Early years input:	*Early years input:*
School years input:	*School years input:*
Literacy plan:	*Literacy plan:*
Special issues:	*Special issues:*

Worksheet 5: School Choice Template

Choosing a school is critical and can be challenging, when parents have the luxury of a choice. Do some research on each school and, to the best of your ability, note expected pros and cons. Based on that information, predict the language outcomes for your child(ren). Compare those with your goals and Family Language Plan to select the best school match.

Name of child:
Language goals:

Pre-school and primary years

Option 1:		Option 2:		Option 3:	
Pros	*Cons*	*Pros*	*Cons*	*Pros*	*Cons*
Predicted language outcomes:		Predicted language outcomes:		Predicted language outcomes:	

Secondary school years

Option 1:		Option 2:		Option 3:	
Pros	*Cons*	*Pros*	*Cons*	*Pros*	*Cons*
Predicted language outcomes:		Predicted language outcomes:		Predicted language outcomes:	

3 Supporting Your Family Language Plan

In this section we will explore the critical conversations that will support your Family Language Plan, and how our knowledge building will provide us with the tools to guide others in supporting our children's bilingual journey. We will start with the importance of family language conversations, between parents and with children. We will then discuss critical conversations with others who are a part of our Family Language Plan, and we will conclude with a discussion on knowing when to get help for our children and what kind of help we might need.

Conversations with Your Children

Why bi/multilingualism?

Among all the important conversations you will have about bi/multilingualism, the ongoing conversation with your children is the most important. In many families, parents wait until the children are older to start the discussion, but in fact this conversation should be started from very early on. Ultimately, parents may make the choices but children have to do the real work. It is important that they feel included in the process and understand the reasons behind the expectations of their parents. As the language conversation evolves, it should encompass issues of heritage, family ties, travel, schooling, local integration or any other factor that impacts the Family Language Plan. Whichever factors are emphasised, the critical issue is to transmit to the children the reasons why they are being asked to learn each language, and to find ways to help them experience each language as a living, useful, dynamic way of communicating.

Early conversations with your children about bi/multilingualism will focus less on why they have more than one language and more on the practicalities of living in a bi/multilingual environment. Even very young children tune in quickly to the language needs of those around them, and by the age of two to three years children can reliably make the right language choices for different people, given adequate input. In the very early years, the family discussion about bi/multilingualism will be framed in terms a young child can understand – 'Mummy says …' and 'Daddy says …' – or whatever the language roles are in the particular situation. By the age of two to three years old, most (bi/multilingual) children have enough awareness of different languages to give them the correct name, but each family can choose the terminology that suits them.

Language status

Different languages carry different value in any society. What is a high-status language in one location many be a low-status language in another. For children to be successfully bi/multilingual in languages that have different apparent value where they live, they must be exposed early and often to the necessity for each of their languages. Parents who speak a minority language (for example, Spanish in the United States) often face more resistance from their children once they are old enough to understand the status and dominance of English. The best tool to combat this kind of negative message is for the family to actively promote the status of all the languages they use, and to engage their community to do the same. For families with limited exposure to one of the languages, this can mean finding means of promoting the language through monolingual tools, and building ties with speakers of that language, either locally or via multimedia sources.

It is also important for parents and family members to be open about their feelings about languages and why different languages are important for different people. This includes discussions about where you are from, what language(s) your parents spoke to you and how those languages are important to you. If you are a parent who uses a minority language with your children but they know you also speak the majority language, it's important to contextualise for them the *why* of your language choices. You can bring into the discussion your family history, including identifying on a map where you/your language are from, and connecting this understanding to the language used when visiting with family, if extended family also use the minority language. Many families I have worked with use the identifier 'language of my heart' with young children, to help them understand how a language has an affective function as well as a communicative function. This affective function will be why a parent persists in using their own language when the majority language would be simpler for all.

Language choices

Language use carries with it many messages that parents might not have considered. Every time a parent uses one language over another, they send their children messages about the value of each language, and perhaps even the cultures attached to those languages. By discussing with children why we make the language choices we do, we help them understand how we value each of the languages we use, and why they are important for the children to acquire. This discussion can start from a very young age – children can differentiate the languages in their environment very early, so it's never too soon to start explaining the language choices of the adults in their world and their expectations for the children. From my work with families over the years, it is clear that families in which the mother speaks a minority language and the father speaks a majority language are in the most difficult situation for raising children with both languages. This intersection of gender and language status is even more problematic when the family has traditional roles as well, with the mother staying at home with the children and the father working outside the home. This particular dynamic often sends the children the message that the mother's language is less important or useful (and therefore of lower status) than the father's language.

While in the early years there is an advantage for the minority language speaking parent who spends more time with the children, this advantage is often offset by the dominance of the majority language when the children start school. The message the children receive once they start school is that their mother's language is not useful outside the house, and that the father's language, the majority language, is the language with status. This is especially the case where the mother also speaks the majority language and it is the language of communication between the parents. (As an aside, I do not know of any research on how this would be the same/different in families with two parents of the same gender.) The message about language status comes through clearly in the facts of the situation, and children will and do pick up on this message: that one language is more important than the other. Over the years I've observed the effects on children in different ways, and while these stories make some of the funniest stories from my work on families, they are also poignant in their effects on families and children.

Stories from children about language status and use

Several years ago I worked with a family with a Russian mother and Dutch father, living in the Netherlands. At six years old, the daughter started refusing to speak Russian. When questioned, she explained to me that 'Russian is a secret language'. She came to this conclusion because her mother only used Russian with her when they were alone; whenever anyone else walked into the room, the mother would switch to Dutch. Because the family had never had a discussion about bilingualism and language use, 'Russian is a secret language' was the conclusion that the child came to, from observing her mother's language use patterns.

A second cautionary tale related to an adult male I met in the Netherlands some years ago. He had been raised by a Dutch mother and a Greek father, in Greece. They had little interaction with other Dutch speakers other than some female friends of his mother. Until he was ten years old he thought only women spoke Dutch, so when he was seven years old he quit speaking Dutch altogether because it was a 'women's language'. When I met him, he had moved to the Netherlands to try and learn Dutch because he had lost most of his Dutch in those younger years. While he was finding it challenging, it is still easier to build on a language that you had as a child than to learn from scratch.

Along with continuing conversations to build understanding of language status within families, adopting a full or partial domains of use approach can be effective as well. Even if the majority language speaking parent hasn't mastered the minority language, they can still be supportive of their children's efforts. This can take the form of family language dinners where the whole family do their best to use the minority language, or 'language lessons' where the children teach some of the minority language to the other parent. The latter is particularly powerful as it sends a dual message about the child as a language expert and the majority language parent as a language learner.

It provides a clear lesson about the value of language and shows that the majority language parent is equally supportive of that language. If the majority language parent is also the main breadwinner and/or the father, their explicit support for the minority language and the minority language speaking parent is critical.

Language use between siblings

One of the elements of the Family Language Plan that parents often don't consider until it becomes an issue is sibling language use. With the first child the parents are in the driver's seat when it comes to language use, and make a plan and (hopefully) stick to it. With each additional child there are influences on our plan arising from how our children choose to use language together, and this is most noticeable when the home language differs from the majority community language. While children are young and still at home, they will usually default to the language most used in the home, but as they spend more time in childcare or educational settings, the language of those settings will often become dominant, even if it is different from the home language(s). As children establish a strong 'language of play', it becomes increasingly difficult to encourage them to revert to a minority language for play at home. While we can influence or encourage our children to use the home (minority) language, we cannot mandate or enforce language use between children. In our family, when we brought our twins home from the hospital, my older daughter (almost four-and-a-half years old) announced that she would be speaking to them in English (the majority language) rather than in French (the minority language) as 'English kids are more fun!' (my apologies to the French). She stuck to this decision for many years, and it definitely impacted how both her younger siblings developed in their languages as well.

When you choose not to learn a local language

If you are a family living abroad as expats, you may feel that learning the local language is not worth the time and effort. Some people take this line because they are only going to be in a country for a short time; others simply don't consider the possibility, perhaps because they believe that adults in general can't learn languages well or that they personally can't learn languages well. While as adults we make decisions that make sense for us, we need to also consider the impact of those decisions on our children. In the case of families living abroad and not learning the local language, there can be an impact on the children's understanding of the value and culture of other languages, and of their own role in the place where they live. At its extreme, the tendency of English-speaking families to live abroad without learning the local language can create a neo-colonial tone in families, and be of great detriment to the children's attitudes about learning other languages.

In my time in the Netherlands I met many English-speaking families whose children were born in the Netherlands but who spoke no Dutch whatsoever, either by accident or by design. Most of these children would confidently tell me that you don't actually need to speak Dutch, because *everyone* in the Netherlands speaks English. This is of course not true. In fact, many of these parents actually did want their children to learn

Dutch, had made efforts to register them in Dutch sports teams or other extra-curricular activities and were surprised when the children didn't appear to learn any at Dutch at all. Again, the messages the parents were sending by continuing to use only English were strong and not mitigated by any discussions about language choices. While I'm not saying that every adult has to learn the language of every country they live in, you can take steps to encourage your children to develop healthy attitudes about languages and the country they are in by paying attention to the messages you are sending and by having ongoing conversations about language choice.

Three rules to live by for expat families:

(1) If you are a monolingual family, make every effort to encourage your child to learn the local language. Bi/multilingualism is a positive choice and learning another language will be beneficial to your child in many ways.

(2) If you choose against the local language, for whatever reasons, make sure you transmit to your children positive attitudes about the language and people regardless. At all times, uphold the status of the local language in your family language discussions, to ensure that your children do not acquire a dismissive attitude to 'lesser' languages, which can be a pitfall of a mobile existence.

(3) Talk to them about why they are not learning the language and always be clear with them about why you made this decision. It's where your children live: they need to understand why they don't understand the language.

What will I do with my languages?

Contextualising, in age-appropriate ways, why both/all of a child's languages are necessary is another aspect of the family language discussion. Most children are not naturally very forward thinking, and the younger the child the more this is true. Parents need to give children some kind of immediate and longer term reasons, in age-appropriate ways, for the linguistic journey they are on. With younger children, connecting a lesser used language to real people can enhance not only input but also motivation. Having grandparents read stories over Skype will prepare children for interaction during visits. Designating certain resources to be used in only one language with a connection to a place or person can also be helpful in setting up monolingual situations. For example, if members of your family send you a game from Spain, that game must be played in Spanish (young children will believe this, older children will not!), and then the game goes with you on visits to Spain and continues to be used as a language development tool.

With older children, literacy is a particular challenge. While simultaneous bilinguals can be perceived as developing two languages with no more effort than one, nobody can argue that developing academic literacy in two or three languages isn't more work. How much work it is depends on the languages involved, their connection or distance from each other and the intricacies of literacy in each. Some languages are more straightforward than others in terms of the connection between how things sound and how they are written and some are more complicated. Some languages have unheard but visible elements that are critical to writing accurately (such as the subject-verb agreements in French). Family conversations about the importance of literacy and the goals that are a part of the Family Language Plan are an important element of helping children work towards the goals that parents have set. Having short-term goals, with visible results, can improve motivation for working on literacy. What motivates each individual child will be different, so it is important to consider each of your children as an individual on their journey to literacy. I have met children who are motivated by the promise of a set of Harry Potter books as a reward once they can read them in English. I have also met children who are motivated by certificates, with the opportunity to sit and pass the French government children's language exams being the reward. Whatever works for your children, there is a clear line from setting language goals, making a plan, having family conversations and a collaborative approach to the plan and success.

Conversations with teenagers about language can be the most difficult. It is very common, and in fact often the norm, for teenagers to move away from minority language use and prefer full-time majority language use. In part, this is simply because they often move away from talking with their parents to interacting far more with their peers, and if their peers all speak the majority language there is no social reason for them to use the minority language. Language choices in adolescence can also be linked to developing identity; in these years most young people like to be the same as their peer group and not visibly or audibly different. These will be the years when your children ask you to not use the minority language outside the home or in the home when they have friends over (if they haven't already made this request). They may also feel that the work they need to put in to maintain and develop their other language, especially related to literacy, is just not worth it.

Finding time and space for the minority language can be more challenging, as you simply aren't spending as much time with your teenagers as they get older. Finding a shared activity that is logical in the minority language or a shared topic of conversation, just for a short time but regularly, can help keep lines of communication open. This may be joining a sports team, watching a TV series together or reading mangas; the quality and content of the activity are less important than the shared time. Mostly, remember that if you have given them a strong foundation and keep speaking to them in your language as much as possible (as much as they will tolerate!), the language will be there for them when they want to come back to it. Depending on how long and how emphatically they have refused to use the language, it may take time and effort, but they will be able to bring it back to life.

Talking about language refusal

Unfortunately, many if not most bi/multilingual families go through this crisis at some point. Despite best efforts to provide good and consistent input, despite the ability to use the language if necessary ... most bi/multilingual children, at some point, figure out which language gets them the most effect for the least effort, and choose to use that language, all the time. I've worked with parents who have tried bribery, threats, enticements and the old stand-by, 'I don't understand you'. The bottom line is, once your child figures out that both parents do speak, or at least understand, the majority (or other) language, it's very hard to get them to make the effort to use the less popular language. So, what's a parent to do?

Here are my suggestions. Firstly, don't try to pretend that you don't understand. It usually doesn't work (either they don't believe you or they don't care), and it can cause bad feeling between the parent and child. In the moment when your child is trying to communicate with you, it's important to support that, even if it isn't in the *right* language. In this case, what you can do (although obviously not all the time) is to recast: restate the phrase, in your language, and continue the conversation. This gives them input in your language, but doesn't interrupt the communicative act.

Secondly, work hard to find or create 'monolingual situations' where the child *needs* to use the language in order to be understood, and preferably to play with other children. The reality of playdates is that as parents we often spend time with certain people simply because we have our children in common. Even if you wouldn't normally seek out your language community to socialise with, it's worth it if it helps your child have the motivation to communicate in your language.

Thirdly, continue the discussion with your children about why you do what you do in terms of language. Each person has the right to make their own language decisions, and so you have the right to continue to use your language of choice just as they have the right to use their language of choice. Sometimes, just by keeping an open dialogue and transmitting the message of importance, children will come back to using both or all their languages (in their own time, of course).

And finally, don't feel guilty. If you are doing all you can do to give your children good quality, consistent input in your language, you are doing your best. At the very least they will have a solid foundation in the language when one day they decide it would actually be useful to speak that other language, and at best your consistency and communication will help them come back to your language sooner rather than later.

Talking about being bi/multilingual in a monolingual world

It is particularly challenging raising children to be bi/multilingual in a monolingual world. It is much harder to use a language that excludes when you are the only one doing so. In a multilingual environment, people use languages that others do not understand all the time. They do what they need to communicate with their children and others in the language they feel is right for any situation. In a monolingual environment, it feels very different to be the only person doing something different. I often meet parents who say they try to use their own language with their children in public, but usually veer towards the majority language out of discomfort or guilt. Even though they know that they have nothing to feel bad about, it still feels rude to use other languages in a monolingual environment.

This reality is becoming more obvious in areas where anti-immigration sentiment is riding high, and speaking other languages is at the least disapproved of and at the worst dangerous. This again should be part of the family language discussions – why we use our own languages and why other people sometimes don't approve. Every parent needs to make a decision for themselves about safety concerns relating to other language use, which is a sad statement about the world today. But even if, and especially if, you choose to speak the majority language outside the home, make sure you talk about it with your children and, if your spouse is a majority language speaker, that they are a part of these conversations as well. In this way your children won't conflate your choices with what is right, but simply with what you feel you need to do.

Talking about accents

When we live in a multilingual world, every comment and criticism we make about language, language use and speakers of other languages is a learning situation for our children. If we comment on someone's accent, it cues in to our children that accent is important and somehow hierarchical. Our children learn their attitudes about language mostly from us – if we show a good example of inclusiveness and acceptance, chances are that our children will pick that up. If we evaluate, criticise or categorise, our children will do the same.

So, we all have a responsibility to think carefully about how we speak about other languages, other language speakers and other accents *before* we make a comment in front of our children about how someone speaks a language that is not their own. After all, an accent is not inherently a negative thing – it's a marker of where in the language world we come from, a marker of our culture and heritage and, above all, an indication that we are making an effort to speak a language that we are not a native speaker of. Surely that should be lauded and not criticised?

Talking about bi/multilingualism in the summer holidays

Summer holidays can be a boon or a bane for bi/multilingual families. For some, it means an opportunity to go on vacation to a country where one of their languages is spoken. For families who can manage regular travel to a place where the minority language is spoken, this can be a valuable tool for helping children to develop in the minority language. Although it can be restrictive to always go to the same place for holidays, the benefits for the children of having an immersion vacation are immense. As children get older (and their school friends become more important than their parents) it can be difficult to encourage them to continue in meaningful communication in the home language. The opportunity to live in the culture, even for just a couple of weeks, reinforces the usefulness of the minority language. The more varied the activity plan the better, as it is good to allow children to interact with family members, to use the minority language in public places and to play with other children who only speak the minority language. These invaluable interactions help bolster the language skills of children who are at risk of becoming passive users of one of their languages. So, if you have a minority language in your family and it is at all possible to go 'home' for the summer, or somewhere that the home language is spoken, take the chance – you won't be disappointed in the results.

On the flip side, there are families where the language that needs continued development is the school language (see p. 57). For these families, maintaining the usage of the school language over the holidays is important, especially if it competes with English (an unfair competition!). It takes a concerted effort for parents to find ways to engage in the minority language during the holidays, especially with young children. When children are literate, simply having them read consistently during the school holidays will help them stay on track and not experience the summer fall-back.

Summary: Conversations with Your Partner and Children

In this section we looked at some of the issues that can arise in bi/multilingual families when the family language dynamic is not an ongoing subject of discussion. Important points to keep in mind are:

- Parents need to be supportive of each other's languages and aligned in their priorities.
- Discussions with children can start from a very young age and continue to grow and change as they get older.
- These discussions should include why each language is important and how it can/will be used.
- Parents cannot force their children to use the 'right' language at all times, but can include the children/teenagers in collaborative discussions about language use.

Conversations with Other People

Besides the parents, there are many other people who play important roles in children's linguistic landscapes. The job of parents is to interact with these people and engage their support and cooperation for their children's linguistic journey. This is one of the main reasons why parents raising bilingual children need to have a knowledge base regarding bilingual development, and a clear plan. Without these two things, decisions will be made without understanding impact, and the opinions of others may sway you away from what you think to be right. You may very well meet other people – professionals or just friends or family – who question your decisions. Your job is to promote the benefits of bi/multilingualism, for your child and for your family, and to advocate for the right help, resources or assessments for your child.

There are many places along the bi/multilingual road where you may question yourself and your decisions. You may need to intervene with teachers who do not understand how your child's bi/multilingual mind works, you may be up against community language school teachers who do not use methods that are sympathetic to their bi/multilingual pupils or you may be opposed by family members who feel that one language is more 'important' than the other. Your best resource in all these cases is accurate information, your dedication to successful bi/multilingualism for your children and your willingness to advocate for them. While the opinions of family and friends may be tiresome on occasion, there is a more pressing issue for parents of young children. One basic truism is that the majority of people involved with children as professionals rarely get any training regarding bilingual development. This includes healthcare professionals, speech therapists, educational psychologists, nursery workers and primary school teachers. Some of these professionals will have had some training in child language development, but generally only in terms of the normal trajectories for monolingual children.

In this section we will look at having conversations with both supporters and naysayers, whether they are within your family or taking care of your children in some official capacity. There are also a series of examples designed to be shared with different professionals, to help them understand how to best to support bilingual children.

Family and Friends

Family

One of the most valuable sources of support we can tap into comes from within families. Getting the best outcomes for our children relies on the parents working in partnership, supporting one another's languages. This partnership is not always easy, especially if the parents didn't set out with a plan. I've met many families over the years in real distress due to language issues, with one partner feeling unsupported or undermined by the other parent. The important conversations we have as co-parents and partners in this journey are the most vital, as we need to be in agreement with each other in order to work successfully with others. This is also true when parents are separated or divorced, which can impact our children's bilingual development in different ways. This is why goal setting is so important; parents need to talk through the language options available and agree on priorities. Having the conversation once doesn't guarantee success, though: it's just the first step. When difficulties arise along the way, going back to that conversation, revisiting the priorities and goals and adjusting if necessary is key to any Family Language Plan.

Extended family

Extended family can impact children's language choices in positive or negative ways. Having an ongoing discussion with family members who are a part of your plan will help them to be supportive, even if they don't initially agree with the decision for bi/multilingualism. Share your language goals and the Family Language Plan as well as what role you would like them to play. Using your knowledge from learning the theory of bi/multilingualism, you can help family members understand their role in the process, whether simply as a supportive cheerleader or as a critical source of adequate input for a minority language. Getting the best support for your children's language development can mean being clear with family members about the key aspects of language acquisition, especially if time with family is a key part of passing on a minority language. The clearer you are about what types of activities would be helpful to provide high-quality input, the better the chance of success. This is not only about linguistic success, but the more language develops between your children and their extended family, the closer their relationships will develop as well. Grandparents can be key funds of knowledge about a country and a culture, and transmitting this through the associated language is beneficial for everyone.

Friends

Many families living internationally have little support for language development from their families except at holiday times. In their absence, creating a language community with friends can be key to success. Although we don't need or want to only socialise with people who only speak our language, the support of friends is immensely helpful when we are trying to pass a minority language on to our children. When children are very young, spending time with other families with young children of the same language background will provide additional input from adults, which is valuable. The opportunity to play with other children who speak the language will help your children develop play-appropriate language that they do not necessarily get from adults. There is often a limit to how long children will use the minority language among themselves; if they are all schooled in the majority language they will quickly catch on and most will switch to using that language for play. Conversations with friends about what resources they are using, creating book-sharing libraries and simply having other parents to help along the way is an important part of a successful minority language plan.

Caregivers and Educators

Caregivers

Throughout the bi/multilingual journey, your children will have many other important sources of linguistic input. The first source from outside the family may be caregivers who look after your children while you are at work. Whether this is an in-home nanny or a daycare-type setting, the more hours your child spends with a caregiver, the more important they become in your Family Language Plan. For some families, the caregiver language is also spoken by one parent. In these cases, their input will provide enrichment but isn't critical to language development. For other families, the caregiver will be the main source of a language that is part of the Family Language Plan but is not spoken in the home. Conversations about expectations will build a sense of partnership, with the caregivers understanding the role that they play in your Family Language Plan. Through this understanding, they are more likely to use the appropriate language (rather than switch, if they can, to the home language), and to provide your child with high-quality input during their time with them.

Unfortunately, very few daycare or early childhood education programmes address child bi/multilingualism. This means that your children's caregivers may at some points not understand the bi/multilingual mind and development. Once again, by providing accurate information and demonstrating clear-cut goals and expectations from all involved, you will be better able to help educate professionals who underestimate or make incorrect assumptions about your children's language development. Bi/multilinguals are not simply two monolinguals in one brain, but a hybrid of their languages and experiences. Caregivers' expectations need to take into account the bi/multilingual experience, and they should be encouraged to inform themselves about best practice for teaching bi/multilingual children.

Language-specific caregivers

As mentioned in the planning section, some families have the expectation that their child(ren) will learn a new language through a childcare situation. In many cases these are immigrant or expat parents choosing a local (community) language daycare or caregiver. As we also discussed in the planning section, this method is not always successful for a variety of reasons. Some families who place a high priority on a language that they cannot pass on themselves will hire a caregiver specifically to be responsible for development in an additional language. This can be in the local (community) language, or it can be in another language not related to the family or location.

I have noticed a growing tendency for monolingual parents to hire a caregiver specifically to help their child become bilingual, in a monolingual environment. Which language they choose varies, but in my experience the choice is often driven by economic factors rather than cultural. This has led to increasing numbers of families hiring Mandarin-speaking caregivers due to the perceived economic value of speaking Mandarin, rather than a language spoken in their community environment. If you are hiring a caregiver specifically to be the main input in an additional language, it's important to give them support in understanding what kinds of things they should do with your child to give them the best possibility of success. How well this works in the short term will be mediated by how much input will be needed to acquire full academic fluency and literacy in later childhood and adolescence. No matter what your goal, ongoing conversations about their role in your language plan and support in understanding how to meet those expectations will provide the best chance of success.

Many parents decide that in order to reach their language goals they need to find additional sources of input in a minority language. I often get asked about hiring language teachers to tutor children, even very young ones. While I completely agree that additional input in a minority language, especially from other people, is a good thing, I don't necessarily think that language tutors are the right way to go about it. Tutors often take a very classroom-oriented approach to their work, essentially viewing their job as private teaching. While this may eventually be valuable for literacy, it isn't necessary with younger children.

The best motivation for young children is older children to play with. Finding a local teenager who speaks the minority language and having them come over for playdates a few times a week is a very successful way not only to provide new and interesting input in language, but also to motivate children to use the minority language. While I don't recommend that parents lie to the children and pretend not to understand them, I think that it is fine for a new person to present as monolingual. This is one way of creating the monolingual situations that are so necessary to provoke output in a less used language. If you are hiring a teenager to come over and play, you need to be very specific about what that means. Again, ongoing conversations about resources to use (favourite games and books, imaginative play) are an important part of success. While you don't need to dictate what they do, and in fact what they do should be child-led, you need to be clear that the goal is language development so constant conversation is a part of their job. This type of 'language tutor' is often more successful because it is led by the child's interests rather than a teaching agenda, and the older child–younger child interactions are very motivating. It is also considerably less expensive than hiring a tutor!

Educators

Conversations with the people who are responsible for your child's education will comprise a large part of your work advocating for your bi/multilingual child. Whether it is to give them accurate information about bilingual development or to better understand how you can help your child at home, these conversations will be ongoing during your child's years at school. As mentioned in the section on school-based bilingualism, a successful pathway to bilingualism through education is based on the parent–school partnership which should be developed and maintained over the years.

The first important conversation is about your child's language profile and language pathway. Teachers (and school administrators) need to know what languages are a part of your child's environment and how important they are, relatively. Identifying for the school what your child's dominant language is on entry will give them insight into how best to support your child, whether it is by assigning them a language buddy who speaks the same language or by encouraging use of translation devices to make sure that your child can understand and be understood.

The second conversation will continue over a whole year with a teacher, and will be based around sharing goals for learning and agreeing on what you, as parents, can do to support curricular learning. Some schools have well-developed systems for sharing upcoming focus areas with parents through online platforms or documents sent home regularly. These enable parents to know what topics their children are learning about, so they can support knowledge development at home, through the dominant language. Through regular discussions, you should be able to gain insight into what your child has understood at school and what they might have missed. Through communicating with the teacher about these areas, you can request additional help for learning or resources that you can use at home. Something as simple as looking at key vocabulary in the dominant language can provide a springboard for the classroom learning around that vocabulary.

It is sometimes necessary and helpful to remind educators of the 'two hats' analogy, especially in the area of assessment. Although it is not usually stated, the implication in all assessment is that it is in the school language. So if they are assessing understanding of an ecosystem, we can identify that they are actually assessing the following: 'Can the student accurately describe how an ecosystem functions, *in English*?' Teachers sometimes forget that implicit expectation, but it is important to remember that a bi/multilingual child will always have knowledge that they cannot (yet) express in the school language during the language development phase. Discussions around how you can support your child in preparing for assessments, or how the school will differentiate assessments to allow for their language learner status, will mean that your child is not consistently assessed inadequately.

A final discussion with the school should be around how you can help them support visible multilingualism and positive attitudes in the school. Language learners thrive in environments that celebrate their unique profiles and make visible their abilities. Home language story time, reading buddies, after-school home language study groups for older children – all of these can be made possible if parents and schools work together to provide the best educational experiences for their multilingual children.

Using the 'Second Language' at Home: What's the Etiquette?

This is a question from a reader, but one that I think may be of interest to many minority language parents. A Greek couple have just moved to the UK with their young son (almost three years old). They are being encouraged by the nursery to use English at home with him, to help him 'learn English faster', and are wondering what they should do about this. It's always a tricky thing to deal with – when educators are telling you to do one thing for your child's good, and you feel that the opposite is better. How do you work around this? Whose responsibility is it to 'teach' the second language? How will it affect the minority language if the parents start using the majority language (in this case, English) in the home? Will it confuse the child or help? Here are some things to consider when making these decisions.

Firstly, you must consider the age and development of your child. If your child understands that there are two different languages and can discuss this with you (even in a basic way, like 'This is *kaas* in Dutch and in English we say *cheese*'), then they are likely to be able to handle their parents changing language with them. So, you could offer some sentences or words in Greek and then say them in English too. However, there are two drawbacks to this method. To begin with, it may not work. If the child has the choice of listening in the language they know best or trying harder in a new language, guess which choice they usually make? Yes, of course, they may just block out the unfamiliar English input and focus on the Greek. You could push the issue, but then you put yourself in the position of creating conflict between your child's two languages. The second issue is that when parents start using the majority language they can be stepping on a slippery slope: as the child gets older and more confident in English, they may stop wanting to use the minority language (Greek) with the parents. Because, after all, the parents started using English with them first.

Another issue to consider is how good the child's first language development is at that moment. A child who is still in the process of acquiring the first language accurately (this is a lifelong process, but the critical years are up to about four years old) needs the continued quantity and quality of input provided by the parents. This is necessary to provide the child with a solid, well-developed first/home language. If the parents start prioritising the new language to the detriment of this language, this can have disastrous consequences for the child.

So, all of this points to the answer to the initial question being that the parents should not start using English at home. How, then, should you deal with the issues brought up by (and suggestions from) the nursery? Firstly, you need to let the nursery know that your intentions are to raise your child as *bi/multilingual*, which means that Greek is just as important as English. And that, developmentally, your child needs to continue to grow in Greek, which will help their English grow as well (see p. 47). Secondly, you can agree with the nursery staff on some critical communicative points that you will help your child to understand. Pictures around the classroom can be very helpful for children who can't yet communicate but who need to express certain ideas. Nurseries that have non-native speaker children should have a system to help pre-verbal children communicate their needs. With parental help to show and talk about these resources in the classroom, the parents can use the home/dominant language – the strongest language – to help children acquire knowledge of classroom routines, etc., for which they then can learn the new words more easily.

As children become more aware of their two languages, and able to translate/differentiate between them, parents can choose to use the majority language sometimes at home. They can create 'domains of use' in which they use English together with the child, to help them learn some basic skills (turn-taking in games, for example) and vocabulary in English. These should be well delineated in time and space ('we are going to sit at the table every Saturday afternoon and play this game in English') to make sure that the child understands that this is a language-based activity and not a lifestyle change.

The bottom line is that children can learn another language by the 'immersion' (or submersion) method, even when they start at later ages. The parents' main job is to support the growth of the home language(s) and by doing so support their child's cognitive development. If they feel that their child is ready, developmentally, to understand the use of two languages at home (in well-defined situations), then they can choose to do this. They can always support nursery learning by talking about all things nursery-related in the home language(s), to help the child understand what they are/should be doing while at nursery.

The job of the nursery staff is to provide resources for pre-verbal children to use in the classroom, and to indicate to the parents (via handouts or email, etc.) what important concepts/routines they want the children to understand in order to be able to participate in class. And if everybody does their job, then the children will come out as successful bi/multilinguals, which should always be the 'end of the road' goal.

Talking to Baby Nurses and Other Medical Professionals

Depending on where you live, you may encounter a variety of professionals when your child is young who are tasked with checking growth and development and ensuring that your child is on track. This may be a special baby clinic, a nurse or a paediatrician. Whatever the system, there is a greater than average chance that they will not know very much, if anything, about bilingualism.

One of the areas of development they will likely track is language development. This may take different forms, but it often simply consists of asking parents to report how many words a child can say. When my children were at this phase of life, we had very different experiences. The clinic my oldest went to had a doctor who knew quite a lot about bi/multilingualism and was happy to have my daughter respond in whichever language was more comfortable for her (in her three-year-old eye test she used English, French and Dutch words). We had a great experience and never felt any pressure to do things differently with her. With my twins we had a different experience. For whatever reason, the doctor we saw regularly was not very supportive of bi/multilingualism. The conversations about language development would always include questions like 'Are you sure three isn't too much for them?' and 'Do they have the same number of words in all three languages? They should, you know'. Fortunately, I was confident in our language decisions and language plan for our children, and her comments never made me worry. However, I've known many parents who ended up questioning themselves and their family language goals when faced with scepticism from medical professionals. I've met families who dropped a language and all became monolingual after being alarmed by advice from doctors or other medical professionals.

It's important to keep in mind that doctors do not study child language development as part of their medical training and neither do nurses. Any opinions they offer you (unless they have had outside training) are based on their personal opinions and experiences.

As parents choosing bi/multilingualism for your children, you should be prepared to question any advice you get (Why do you believe that? What training have you had in this area?) and make your own decisions, based on your family situation and your research. So, if needed, don't be afraid to advocate for your child.

In defence of the bi/multilingual child

These three phrases, and the knowledge behind them, could be the most important tools parents have when advocating for their bi/multilingual child:

(1) *'His/her language development is on target for bi/multilingual acquisition. Would you like me to give you some resources to read about this topic?'* This phrase demonstrates that you are not susceptible to fear-based tactics and that you are following your child's language development closely. In addition, it shows that you have knowledge about the topic and have actual information behind your statements. And it shows that you are happy to be helpful and share the information with them.

(2) *'Research demonstrates that bi/multilingualism has many benefits for children. Would you like me to give you some resources to read about this topic?'* 'Research demonstrates' is a powerful phrase when going up against health and education professionals. If you know what research says about bi/multilingualism, and aren't afraid to tell them, they will most likely defer to you rather than persist in trying to advise you. And, of course, you can helpfully offer to share the information with them, in case they really are interested in learning something.

(3) *'No, we are not worried. We have a Family Language Plan for our children, based on the latest research. Would you like me to give you some resources to read about this topic?'* This demonstrates that you are playing an active role in your child's language journey, and the word 'plan' shows that you are serious about what you are doing. When you throw 'research' in there, it helps give you gravitas … and of course, ever helpful, you can offer to share your information with them.

Summary: Conversations with Other People

In this section we have looked at different conversations we may have with people who are a part of our Family Language Plan, and the conversations we may need to have with people who are not supportive of our plan and our children's bilingual development.

Some points to remember are:

- Family and friends will not always act in ways that are supportive of our Family Language Plan unless we are specific about what role they play.
- Conversations with caregivers about their role will help them best support our children.
- Be aware that most childcare and medical professionals do not get formal training in bi/multilingual development, so if they offer you advice, be sure to do your research before following it.

- *A Parents' and Teachers' Guide to Bilingualism* (Baker, 2014) is useful for sharing information with others, as each question/section is concise and easy to read.

Resources to Share with Your Child's School

Supporting home languages (everyone's!) at school

Research clearly shows that allowing or encouraging children to use their home languages at school is not detrimental to learning the school language and can be beneficial for various reasons. Building on a child's prior knowledge and linguistic expertise in their own language is key to success for bilingual learners. Supporting home language use also supports children's sense of self, confidence and integration into the school community. A child's home language(s) is a fundamental part of who they are and where they are from, and to cut them off from that in their learning environment is not acceptable.

Here are some ways in which schools can embrace the challenge of languages and support all their learners:

(1) *Bi/multilingualism is beneficial to children.* This means all children, no matter what two (or more) languages are involved, and even if one or more of these are minor languages, or dialects or not really 'useful'. All too often, bi/multilingualism is regarded as desirable and worth working for if the children are middle or upper class and the languages are high status, but it is frequently viewed as a 'problem' if the children are from immigrant or refugee families and speak a low-status language at home. The brain does not differentiate between high- and low-status languages, and bi/multilingualism should be supported at school no matter who the children are or what their home languages are.
(2) *Let the children use their languages, for socialising and for learning.* If you make their language something 'bad', they will use it in this way. I hear all the time, 'but when they use their own language it is to mock or exclude', as an excuse for banning any other languages in school. If children are forbidden from using their language because it is considered unwelcome, not as good or even 'bad', then they will use their language to prove what they are being told. In schools where language diversity is embraced and encouraged there are fewer language-related problems, because all the children feel accepted and use their languages in more positive ways because of it.
(3) *Integrate knowledge about language across the curriculum.* You don't have to be multilingual yourself to discuss how languages work. The school language is talked about all the time, but let the other-language speakers talk about their home languages when language is being discussed. A conversation about how pronouns work in English can be enriched by comparing how pronouns work in other languages – for all the learners, including the monolinguals.
(4) *Use translanguaging* – the alternation of home and school languages – as a pedagogical tool to help your minority language speakers thrive. Also known as 'dynamic multilingualism', this strategy for deepening learning and improving language, both home languages and school language, is growing in prominence in research and

literature about multilingualism in schools. Translanguaging is a practice that plans for the use of home languages in the classroom, so that early emergent bi/multilinguals can understand and learn better and later emergent bi/multilinguals can continue to grow in their home languages by using them to mediate academic content.

Schools that enrol large numbers of non-native pupils, whether they are high-status international schools or regular state schools, have a duty to understand the needs of these learners and provide for their growth and learning in ways that respect the whole child, including their own languages.

Resources to Share with Baby Nurses or Other Medical Professionals

This is a template that you can use to create a letter of introduction to share with anyone who will be interacting with you and your child in a medical or educational capacity.

Dear ...

We are delighted to be raising our child as a bi/multilingual. We have done our homework on the topic, and have developed a Family Language Plan. In doing the research, we have found the following important information about young bilinguals, which we think is important in understanding our child. We are sharing it with you because you are a part of our child's life and also need to have accurate information about their development. These are what we think are the most important things to understand about developing language in young bilinguals:

(1) Bilingualism is normal, and babies and young children all over the world are raised with more than one language, with no detrimental effects.
(2) We have chosen the following languages for our child:

    (a)   Language 1
    (b)   Language 2
    (c)   Language 3

(3) In the early years of developing bilingualism, it is normal for babies/toddlers to have different vocabulary in each language. As long as the combined vocabulary count is within the normal range, there is no cause for concern. This means that any language assessment will need to consider all languages.
(4) Children being raised with more than one language are at no greater risk of speech or language delays, or other educational challenges. If a child does have speech or other challenges, they can still successfully become bilingual; dropping a language is not necessary or generally advisable.

We would be happy to discuss our research or share further resources about any of these points with you.

Thank you for your time.

Worksheet 6: Conversations with Your Children

What are the reasons why your child(ren) are being asked to learn another language? In the worksheet provided, note your reasons, including any reasons that are unique for different languages. Note the name and age of each child (their age will determine how you communicate the reason). For each reason, note some age-appropriate conversation ideas. Think about what motivates each child and note an activity or other motivator to include in your conversations.

Reasons: Language 1	Child's name and age:	Child's name and age:
Reasons: Language 2	Child's name and age:	Child's name and age:
Motivator for:	Motivator for:	

Worksheet 7: Conversations with Other Key People

Before starting this final worksheet, review your work on all the preceding worksheets. What were your reasons for choosing bi/multilingualism on Worksheet 1? Review the rationales for your goals on Worksheet 3. Go back to your Family Language Plan (Worksheet 4) and review the notes you made on special issues. Look at your ideas for language inputs. Finally, review your notes on your school of choice, including the pros and cons of that school.

For each key person supporting or involved with your child's language learning, note the things you will need to discuss with them, whether a special issue, your plan for language inputs or your goals. What are the most important items to discuss with each person, either because they can provide support or because they will have influence or impact? Using your reasons and rationales, along with the theory and information you have learned in this book, note what you will need to discuss with each person, including how they can help and what they need to know in order to help your child to be successful. Write out your expectations for each person (or category of key people).

Family	
Goal(s):	*Language input(s)*
Special issue(s):	*Expectation(s)*
Friends	
Goal(s):	*Language input(s)*

Special issue(s):	Expectation(s)

Caregivers	
Goal(s):	Language input(s)
Special issue(s):	Expectation(s)

Educators	
Goal(s):	Language input(s)
Special issue(s):	Expectation(s)

Know When to Get Help

> Practically speaking, there is no empirical evidence at present to justify restricting children with developmental disorders from learning two languages. (Genesee, 2015: 12)

While bilingualism does not cause language delays or learning difficulties, bilingual children can encounter a number of obstacles to successful language development. Some of these may be specific to multiple language acquisition and some may be related to their overall development. We know that children with different challenges can and do become successfully bilingual, but knowing when to get help, and what kind of help to get, is important. In this section we will look at:

- Indicators that you may need to seek out professional help
- What kind of help you might need
- How to find the right professional for your family

Bilingualism-specific Help

Family language planning can sometimes be challenging, and implementing a plan even more so. Parents may benefit from consulting a specialist in bilingualism, to make sure their plans are appropriate, to evaluate a child's progress, to prepare documentation for teachers or for other services. If you face difficulties or uncertainties it can be helpful to consult someone with specialised knowledge in both theory and practice. This route can be useful if you feel that your child is really only using one language and isn't developing the second/other language alongside, or if you are having difficulty identifying appropriate language goals or support resources. A professional with training in bilingual development and experience working with families may be able to help you identify ways and means to adjust your Family Language Plan in order to work better towards your goals. This can be as simple as identifying input needs or helping to plan for a structured enhanced input for a lesser used language. In all cases, they can help parents understand what elements are within their control in terms of maximising their children's potential. Professional support can also be useful in advocating for appropriate school support or in understanding school options and pathways to bilingual success.

How do you find a qualified bilingualism expert?

On a first glance at a Google search, it may look as if it is quite easy to find a 'bilingual expert' to help you on your journey. Unfortunately, there are no clear qualifications for this kind of work, so the vast majority of people selling their services are not actually qualified in any way. In my work with families I draw on my knowledge base from education, in terms of understanding child development, normal and atypical language development and educational psychology. I also draw on my knowledge from years of language teaching and understanding how to plan for and track language development, as well as knowledge about many different school systems and curricula. My expertise in bilingual development comes from graduate work in applied linguistics, including bilingualism in development and sociolinguistics, with an understanding of language variation, language status and other related issues. While this may look like an extensive list of topics to be knowledgeable about, working with families on language planning can be an incredibly complex endeavour and may include many of these areas.

When considering any particular professional to work with, I would advise looking closely at their qualifications. An expert with a background in teaching, especially with multilingual learners, or with experience in any kind of therapeutic background (speech and language therapy, child development, psychology) with experience working with bilingual children would be your best choice, as they will be most likely to have a combination of knowledge about child development and knowledge of bilingual development.

Language development or language delay: When should we worry?

One of the most difficult questions I get asked is: How can parents know what is natural language development and what might be a language delay?

The simple answer is that there is no simple answer. Differentiating between types of language issues can be tricky, even for professionals. The one thing we do know is that raising children with more than one language *does not* cause a language delay. It's often quoted that bilingual children start talking later than monolingual children, but for children with typical language development this is not true. As mentioned in the first section, the different language development trajectories of bilingual children can be misinterpreted as a language delay simply because they have fewer words in each language. This deficit model of bilingualism is based on wrongly comparing bi/multilingual children to monolinguals: if they don't have the same numbers of words/language ability as a monolingual of the same age, they must have a language delay. In fact, for most bilingual children, if you add the words in both/all of their languages together they actually have more words than monolingual children. Parents who are concerned, or who want to track language development, can access resources that will help them graph what the normal trajectories are in their home language(s), and can keep an eye on their children's progress compared to the development standards.

A cause for concern comes when you realise that your child cannot use any of their languages at an age-appropriate level. Differing development in both/all languages is not an issue in and of itself, but parents should be able to identify their child's dominant (strongest) language, and that language should be within the normal developmental range. If none of their languages is within the normal range for their age, this is a red flag.

Speech and language therapy: Getting it right

There are certainly bilingual children with speech and/or language delays, although not in any greater numbers than monolinguals. Despite this, bi/multilingual children are assessed as having speech and/or language delays in higher numbers, simply because of a lack of understanding of bilingual development. Speech and language issues are related to physiology (the ability to make speech sounds) or neurology (the ability to process and create language). Although these children can still become successful bilinguals, early and appropriate intervention will give them the best chance of success.

What are parents to do if they are concerned about their bilingual child's language development? My professional advice is always to arrange for an evaluation, as soon as possible. The key is not to get *any* evaluation, but to get the *right* evaluation. Ideally, bilingual children should be evaluated by a speech therapist who is bilingual in the same languages. That is, of course, rarely an option, so the second-best option is to find a speech therapist who can evaluate them in their dominant language, and who is knowledgeable about and sympathetic to bilingualism. If a speech therapist in the dominant language is not available, or if you can't identify what the dominant language is/should be, getting separate assessments is also a possibility, or doing a collaborative assessment with the speech therapist working with parents to carry out the assessment in the dominant language. It is important to note that a standard speech evaluation is based on monolingual norms and isn't appropriate for a bilingual child; it will measure their language development only in one language, which does not give a clear picture of the development of a bi/multilingual child.

First and foremost, you need to look for a professional who understands bilingual development, as they will be able to plan the best course of assessment. The benefit of an evaluation is that you will have the information you need to provide the best environment for your bilingual child, whether they have a delay or not. If the child does have a delay, early intervention is ideal, and the family should continue to maintain both languages – removing one language will not fix the problem and could make it worse. Again, working with a therapist who understands bilingual development will allow for planning interventions in both languages, as necessary, either with the therapist or with the parents. At the end of this section there is a list of resources which could be helpful in finding supportive information and therapy.

Educational support

Children who are bilingual can also be faced with a variety of learning challenges that are not caused by, but can be impacted by, their bilingualism (e.g. autism spectrum disorders (ASD), specific language impairment (SLI), attention deficit disorder (ADD) and attention deficit hyperactivity disorder (ADHD), Down's syndrome or others). Although there is no evidence that these children should be raised monolingually, it is important to work with professionals who understand and are supportive of bilingualism to ensure the best outcomes for the children.

Children with known challenges

Some children are born with immediately identified conditions that will cause them to have additional educational challenges. This is the case, for example, with children born with Down's syndrome or other complex syndromes that affect both physical and cognitive growth. Research on specific populations varies, as there are a wide variety of conditions that impact individuals in different ways. For example, consistent research shows that children with Down's syndrome can become as successfully bilingual as their monolingual peers. If families get accurate information quickly enough, the best course is to use the necessary languages from birth, as choosing only one language can cut a child off from whole branches of their family and community. The reality is that children with a multiplicity of challenges are born into multilingual communities all over the world, and learn to use the necessary languages to the best of their ability.

Children with emerging challenges

Some special educational needs (SEN) are not apparent at birth or in infancy but slowly become apparent as children develop. Earlier diagnoses are often recommended and sought for children with significant speech and/or language delays, with early identification being key to receiving proper support. Children with ASD can be diagnosed fairly young for more severe iterations, or later on if the challenges only become more apparent in the school years. The same can be said for SLI, ADD and ADHD. Assessment and diagnosis for dyslexia often only occurs when children are having significant challenges in learning to read and/or write.

What choices are open to you and your child in terms of support for any educational needs as well as bilingualism will depend on where you live. Which choice is the right one, from the ones available to you, will depend on your family language profile and plan, and what support and resources are available. As with finding appropriate speech and language support, finding a qualified educational psychologist with the necessary understanding of bi/multilingual development is key. It is important that educational assessments are carried out in a child's dominant language. Any type of educational assessment for SEN will be inaccurate in a non-dominant language. If your child is in a school where they are also a language learner (of the school language), no assessments should be carried out in the school language for a minimum of three years.

While children with SEN may require more time, they can certainly, with the help of their parents and dedicated and knowledgeable professionals, successfully learn to use more than one language. In all cases, I advise parents to reach out for help as soon as they start to have concerns. The right professional can either put your mind at ease or get your child immediate and accurate help if needed. In either case, parents are saved the stress of worrying 'what if', and of trying to figure things out for themselves. The bibliography for this section has a selection of key readings on different educational challenges and bilingualism.

Bilingualism is not the problem if ...

People (unfortunately, sometimes including specialists) often like to lay the blame for language delays or special educational issues on the doorstep of bilingualism. A child having more than one language is seen, too often, as a 'problem' and therefore language is viewed as the cause of other 'problems'. And of course, if bilingualism is the cause, then the answer is monolingualism – taking away one or more languages is widely (incorrectly) accepted as a quick fix for many problems.

Here is a short list of common claims about bilingualism and language/educational development:

(1) *You are told that your toddler 'doesn't have enough words' and may be delayed because they are bilingual.* Everyone knows that bilingual children start talking later, right? Wrong! Bilingual children do not, on average, develop language later than monolinguals. What they do have is a different vocabulary development trajectory. Bilingual children don't develop a word in each of their languages for the same object, at the same time. They develop words from the contexts in which they hear them. So, if the Spanish-speaking father feeds the child every day, they are likely to have mainly Spanish words for eating-related concepts. If the child goes to daycare in Dutch, they learn appropriate Dutch vocabulary for that situation, and not in Spanish. What often happens is that people (parents, professionals) look at the number of words in one language and declare that the child is slow, or delayed. In fact, until about four years old, you need to look at the total number of words in all languages to get an accurate count. After this age, most bilinguals do actually know 'all the words' (or most of them) in both languages, which would effectively mean that they have double the vocabulary of a monolingual child (but nobody ever talks about that).

(2) *Your child is diagnosed with a speech/language delay and you are told that bilingualism is the cause.* It is not true that being raised bilingual *causes* a speech delay. If a child has a delay in speech and/or language, they would have that same delay even if they were only being raised with one language. Speech and language delays can have many causes, mostly neurological or physiological, but bilingualism is never a *cause* of delay. If you have a child with a diagnosed delay, the best path is therapy through both languages, so that they can improve in both languages. Dropping a language is (almost) never the right choice.

(3) *Your child is diagnosed with special educational needs* (ADHD, ASD, PDD-NOS or other). You are told that having two languages (or more) is 'too much' and that it is affecting your child's behaviour and is the cause of, or contributing to, their diagnosis. Again, not true. It is true that sometimes bilingual children struggle with communication in one of their languages, or show frustration with the process and act out. It is not true that having more than one language causes systemic behavioural or neurological issues. It's also not true that removing a language will fix the 'problem'. It is true that you need to find the right professional to work with a bilingual child in terms of therapy, so that you know that the 'whole child' is being seen, rather than only one side.

(4) *Children with special educational needs can't become bilingual; it's too hard, so don't even bother.* And again, not true. Children with a wide variety of SEN (Down's syndrome, ASD, dyslexia and other cognitive functioning diagnoses) can and do become bilingual, in situations where they need both of their languages. It's a very hard subject to research because every child with SEN is completely individual in their talents and challenges and unique possibilities, but increasingly, research supports the possibility of bi/multilingualism for all children.

In short, threats of delays and disturbances should no longer be a part of the discussion on bilingualism. We need to spread the word that becoming bilingual is not harmful, and that it does not cause our children to be delayed or troubled. We need to recognise that bilingual children are *as likely as* monolingual children to struggle with speech or language delays or with educational challenges. Not *more* likely – *as* likely. And we need to recognise that, just as for any other child facing a challenge, there is no easy solution, and certainly removing a language is not the easy solution many think it will be.

Resources for Parents, Teachers and Professionals

Language assessment and/or therapy resources

Speakaboo (http://www.speakaboo.io/)

Speakaboo is an app that allows speech therapists to assess the speech development of young children (three to six years old) in their dominant home language. There are currently 19 languages available, with more being added in the coming months and years. The app, and the content for the assessments, was created by Royal Dutch Kentalis, a Dutch organisation that specialises in diagnostics, care and education for children and adults who are deaf, hard-of-hearing or deafblind and those who have language impairments. They have used their experience and expertise to create this app which can be used by professionals and parents together, to get an accurate picture of a child's language development and therefore to identify if there are language issues that need addressing. I have recommended Royal Dutch Kentalis to many families over the years, as they fit the mandate of professionals who understand bilingual development; this app is the next step in providing wider support.

TinyEYE (https://tinyeye.eu/language/en/slps/)

Several years ago, I was introduced to a new system of telespeech, an online platform called 'TinyEYE'. TinyEYE was created in Canada, where there are many remote populations where children have no access to speech therapy services. It provides professional services via the internet, with a qualified and trained speech therapist assigned to each child. This is a fantastic development not only for remote populations, but also for the international bilingual community. TinyEYE is now working in Europe, based in the Netherlands. At this time they can offer online therapy in Dutch, English, French, German, Turkish, Irish, Farsi and Spanish, and they are working on translating the materials into other languages. The breadth and depth of the therapy options available through the platform are impressive, as is the tracking system which allows parents, teachers and therapists to collaborate through the platform. An extra bonus is that it is great fun for children, so getting them to participate should be easy. TinyEYE also works with schools, so if your child's school needs access to therapists working in other languages, this could be useful for them too.

Free online courses

The following two free online courses are designed for teachers, but if you are a parent of a bilingual child with speech or language challenges, or a teacher of multilingual students, they could be interesting for you as well. They both have good articles associated with them that provide understanding of the challenges of bi/multilingualism and dyslexia, and also have sections that provide information about strategies and support.

Dystefl course: https://www.futurelearn.com/courses/dyslexia.
Dyslang course: https://www.bdadyslexia.org.uk/services/training/dyslang-dyslexia-
  and-additional-academic-language-learning.

Helpful websites and blogs

These three websites and blogs are all maintained by qualified and experienced speech and language therapists. The information in the blogs is robust and valuable and they also have other links to resources and further information about bilingualism and speech and language delays and disorders.

2 Languages, 2 Worlds: https://2languages2worlds.wordpress.com/.
Bilinguistics Speech Therapy: https://bilinguistics.com/speech-therapy-blog/.
Bilingual Therapies: http://blog.bilingualtherapies.com/.

Research

Professor Fred Genesee (McGill University, Montreal) is the leading researcher in the field of developmental delays and bilingualism. You can find many of his articles online, including this one: https://www.colorincolorado.org/article/risk-learners-and-bilingualism-it-good-idea

Martin, D. (2009) *Language Disabilities in Cultural and Linguistic Diversity*. Bristol:
  Multilingual Matters.

Concluding Remarks

As we conclude, let's take a look back at the building blocks for success, and some important points to take with us.

(1) Raising bilingual or multilingual children is a gift and a challenge. Depending on our family circumstances (languages involved, support network), it may be more or less challenging, but it is always worth the effort to get our children as far as we can with their languages before they need to take responsibility for themselves.

(2) Learning about the theory and research around bi/multilingual development can help us make the best choices and plan for our family and children. You've made it to the end of this book so that is a good start, but there are many ways to continue learning more.

(3) Setting your goals will allow you to plan better for patterns of language use that will be helpful for your children. Without thinking through our goals, we may end up off track and wondering how to get back on. That said, your Family Language Plan will be constantly evolving. It may need to be adapted because of a new child, a family move, a separation or divorce, a necessary change of school or for many other reasons. The key to knowing how to adapt your plan is knowledge about the elements that are necessary for language development to happen.

(4) Having conversations around language use is an important part of activating a Family Language Plan. These may be conversations with your children (especially your teenagers!) or with family members, babysitters or others, but again, the more knowledgeable we are and the more we understand our plan, the better we can communicate about it with others.

(5) Be flexible, patient and encouraging. Our children are on this journey with us, and each of them will bring their own characteristics as well. What works for one child may not do so for another child, and it is normal for children within the same family to end up with different levels of bilingualism even if the family circumstances stay the same. It's also important to be flexible, patient and encouraging between parents. Living in a bi/multilingual family can have its challenges, and if parents are not working together it can be a real source of tension. Both parents need to support one another's languages, at all times, and work together rather than in competition.

(6) Stay the course. At times you may want to throw in the towel and revert to using only one language, as it just doesn't feel like it's worth the effort. Whatever you

build for your children when they are younger will be a basis for them to redevelop their bilingualism when they realise how useful it is (as most do). It's easier to build on the base that your parents gave you than to start from nothing, so it's worth your continuing effort.

And so, we come to the end of the book. I hope that you find the information helpful on your journey to bilingualism with your children, and that it is a successful journey. This book would not have been possible without all of the wonderful parents I have met over the years, who have shared their questions, concerns and family stories with me. I occasionally have a family contact me that I worked with years ago, and I remember the languages and stories if not always the names! It has been a pleasure and a privilege to be part of so many families' stories, and I hope this book will be able to support many more than I can personally work with.

Glossary of Terms

Academic language: Refers to the register of language (oral, written, auditory and visual) that students need to be proficient in to perform academically.

BICS (basic interpersonal communicative skills): Everyday language, usually context-bound and not cognitively challenging. In school situations, it is the language of the playground and social interactions. BICS usually takes one to two years to develop in a full-time immersion situation.

Bilingual education: Education programmes in which two languages or more are present in the curriculum, as languages of instruction.

Bilingualism: The ability to understand and use two or more languages in appropriate contexts and for appropriate purposes.

Biliteracy: The ability to read or write to an academic level (age-appropriate) in two languages.

CALP (cognitive academic language proficiency): Students' ability to understand and express, in both oral and written modes, concepts and ideas that are relevant to success in school, including academic language.

Communicative bilingualism: A level of bilingualism that allows a person to speak/understand the language comfortably.

Community bilingualism: When bilingualism is practised within a community, in systematic ways (e.g. in India, where most people speak at least one local language, as well as Hindi, and sometimes English or other local languages).

Domains: Areas of space (physical or otherwise) in which a certain language is used (e.g. at home, at school, with grandparents).

Domains of use: A strategy bi/multilingual families can use to plan for the development of each language, by planning for certain spaces (physical or otherwise), topics or areas of life according to the language being developed.

Dominant language: The language a student feels most comfortable and confident in at any point. The dominant language can change over time and circumstances, but each student should be age-appropriate in at least their dominant language.

Family language: A language spoken in the nuclear or extended family, usually one that will be passed on to children.

Family Language Plan: A guiding document that families develop in order to set their goals and plan for their children's bi/multilingual development.

First language: The first language, or languages, mastered by a child (formerly called mother tongue).

Home language(s): Language(s) that a child has been exposed to in the home from birth. Often referred to in research as *first language(s)*.

Host country language: The language spoken in a country that a family is living in temporarily.

Immersion education: Education in which the language of instruction is not the language of some or all of the students. Language is expected to be learned through the delivery of content in the target language.

L1: Term used in research to designate the language(s) a child has been exposed to from birth and uses regularly.

L2: Term used in research to designate languages learned after the initial period of language development.

Language acquisition: The process of acquiring or learning (terms are interchangeable) a new language.

Language delay: A communication disorder characterised by a failure to develop language (receptive and/or productive) at an age-appropriate rate. A language delay is a diagnosable condition and is not to be conflated with language acquisition with regards to language learners in schools.

Language status: The perceived socioeconomic, sociocultural and/or political prestige of a language in relation to other languages around it; languages can have high, low or neutral status.

Majority language: The language spoken by most of the people in an environment.

Minority language: A language spoken by some people in an environment but not by most. Minority language is often associated with immigrants or other migrants who arrive in a country as speakers of another language.

MLaH (minority language at home): A strategy bi/multilingual families can use, in which both parents speak the minority language at home and the majority language is used outside the home.

Mother tongue: Formerly used to designate the first or strongest language of a child. Now replaced by first/home language or dominant language.

OPOL (one-parent, one-language): A strategy bi/multilingual families can use, in which parents who have different first/dominant languages each speak their own language to their children.

School language: The language of instruction of the school, generally used when it is different from the home.

Subtractive bilingualism: When learning a second language (through education) has negative effects on the development of the students' first language.

Translanguaging: The use of two (or more) languages in a dynamic way, without concern for 'mixing' but for overall communication. A short video explanation can be found here: https://www.youtube.com/watch?v=iNOtmn2UTzI.

Appendix A: Sample Family Language Plan

Language 1: English Literacy goal	Language 2: German Literacy goal
Early years input: • From Hans at home, from Melina sometimes at home, as the family language. • For Nicholas, in daycare.	*Early years input:* • From Hans at home, from family and community. • For Sophie, in daycare.
School years input: • Continued use of English as the family language, as well as for socialising with friends and community. • Some basic exposure in primary school.	*School years input:* • German school from Year 1 (for Nicholas) and from Kindergarten (for Sophie). • Consider different schooling options for secondary school, such as the bilingual schools, which will help the children attain an academic level of reading and writing in both German and English.
Literacy plan: • The children should continue to be exposed to written/read English at home, and to engage with books in English through 'dialogic reading' with Melina. Remember to ask questions that are abstract, along with concrete, to develop thinking skills in English. • Because English shares an alphabet with German, learning to read and write can be easier. As long as the children have a good level of English and are exposed to English books, you can encourage them slowly to try reading. • The children can be encouraged to try writing in English when they show interest. This would simply be for the experience at the beginning and not for accuracy. • Once the children are comfortably literate in German you can focus more on accuracy in English. • Melina should do homework/talk about school with the children in English and Romanian (not at the same time!), to encourage transfer of knowledge from German to English and Romanian.	*Literacy plan:* • The children should be exposed to written/read German at home as well as at school, and to engage with books in German through 'dialogic reading' with Hans. This is particularly important as the children currently have some time to develop their vocabulary before learning to read in German at school.

Special issues:	*Special issues:* • Both girls could use some extension work on their German, to improve vocabulary. English is currently dominant in the home. It would be beneficial for Hans to use German with both children as much as possible when they are alone, and to read to them every day in German.
Language 3: Romanian Communicative goal	**Language 4: Spanish**
Early years input: • From Melina, and visits with family.	From a nanny, three days a week (mixed with English)
School years input: • From Melina and visits with family. • Recommendations: As the children get older and interested in technology, consider getting Romanian resources (where available), especially learning-type games and literacy activities.	
Literacy plan: • Pre-literacy: The children should be exposed to written/read Romanian as much as possible, and to engage with books in Romanian through reading with Melina. Remember to ask questions that are abstract, along with concrete, to develop thinking skills in Romanian. • Once the children are comfortably literate in the school language, they can start learning literacy skills in Romanian, if you choose. Their ultimate success will depend on their level of spoken Romanian and their individual motivation to learn to read/write in Romanian. Family members can be helpful with this, by sending postcards, emails, etc. to the children, to encourage engagement with the language.	
Special issues: • Romanian is the third language and will be under-represented in terms of amount of input, as only Melina speaks it with the children regularly. • Consider finding other sources of input for Romanian, such as friends, babysitters, teenagers who can play and read once or twice a week. • Eventually, consider switching from school-based after-school care to in-home after-school care so that you can hire a Romanian speaker.	*Spanish:* • The children have had a Spanish-speaking nanny for some years, and have varying levels of receptive and productive Spanish. Because of the complex nature of the three-language situation and the priority to improve input in Romanian, I would not advise attempting to continue with the Spanish at this time.

Notes and comments

Quality of input: In cases where one language gets less time than the other, it can be helpful to plan for high-quality input. This involves directed reading and play in order to use language that encourages 'thinking' in a language. Useful tools are games and puzzles as well as books. Consider aiming for at least 30 minutes of 'quality' Romanian input with each child, each day. When visiting with Romanian-speaking family, encourage them to talk to the children and engage with them as much as possible, through shared activities. These strategies can also be used to help the children's German improve to a more advanced level.

Consider finding ways for the children to be exposed to 'child language' in Romanian, or the language of play, so that they will feel comfortable in the company of other children. Right now, they only get input from adults, so their language for play is limited and they do not see a particular use for the language in their immediate friend groups. Playing with other children will help them to 'grow' their Romanian at an age-appropriate rate.

Creating 'monolingual situations': Nicholas and Sophie may eventually try to use German with Melina, if they move towards dominance in the school language. It is important to continue to engage in monolingual situations, in which only one language (Romanian or English) can be used effectively. This will encourage the continued usefulness of the minority languages.

Family language discussions: It is important to discuss with Nicholas and Sophie why you have more languages in the family, and why you want them to use all their languages. It is also important for both parents to support the use of the other parent's languages, so the girls understand that all the languages belong in their family. Hans is somewhat ambivalent about the role of Romanian in the family, as he considers English to be Melina's dominant language and more useful. However, Melina identifies strongly with her Romanian history, and this needs to be supported, as does her desire to have her children able to connect with this part of their identity. Ongoing discussions and reading (as shared) will help both parents come to align with the goals set in this Family Language Plan.

Appendix B: School Planner

Family: Maria, Ahmed and Lily
Language goals: English: academic literacy; Dutch: communicative; Spanish: communicative/basic literacy; French: basic literacy; Arabic: communicative

Pre-school years

Option 1: Dutch crèche until four years old		Option 2: Dutch crèche until 2.5 years, move to English crèche/preschool		Option 3: Move to English care (in home)	
Pros	*Cons*	*Pros*	*Cons*	*Pros*	*Cons*
• Continue Lily's progress in Dutch, which is apparently already strong. • Give her a strong communicative foundation to feel at home in NL.	• No English input until school age.	• Gives time for English development prior to starting school in English. • Continues growth in Dutch for a while longer.	• Lily will likely lose her Dutch to some extent after moving to English care.	• Begins building English early, which is meant to be the primary academic language.	• Loses progress in Dutch, which will become a secondary language (now is a primary language).

Primary school years

Option 1: Dutch school		Option 2: Bilingual school		Option 3: English school	
Pros	*Cons*	*Pros*	*Cons*	*Pros*	*Cons*
• Integrated as much as possible into the local community. • School is close to home; children seem happy there.	• Less overt support for multilingualism in many Dutch schools (compared to international schools). • Dutch will become main academic language. • Issues with changing school language if you leave after six years.	• Would get both Dutch and English at school, although in a predominantly Dutch environment. • Some support for bilingualism (but not necessarily for the home languages).	• Level of success in teaching English varies by school. • May not be a bilingual school in the local area. • Dutch would be main academic literacy language.	• International school environment with children and families from similar backgrounds. • Would promote English as the primary language of academic literacy. • Could eventually study French as well. • Easy to move to another country.	• Dutch would be supported at a basic level. • Community can be transient. • Transportation/cost.

Bibliography

Adoniu, M., Toner, G. and Lee, M. (2016) *The Potentials of K-12 Literacy Development in the International Baccalaureate PYP and MYP*. The Hague: International Baccalaureate.

Antón, E., Theirry, G. and Duñabeitia, J. (2015) Mixing languages during learning? Testing the one subject-one language rule. *PLoS ONE* 10 (1). See https://doi.org/10.1371/journal.pone.0130069.

Antoniou, K. and Katsos, N. (2017) The effect of childhood multilingualism and bilectalism on implicature understanding. *Applied Psycholinguistics* 38 (4), 787–833.

Antoniou, M. (2019) The advantages of bilingualism debate. *Annual Review of Linguistics* 5 (1), 395–415.

Baker, C. (2011) *Foundations of Bilingual Education and Bilingualism* (5th edn). Bristol: Multilingual Matters.

Baker, C. (2014) *A Parents' and Teachers' Guide to Bilingualism* (4th edn). Bristol: Multilingual Matters.

Baker, C. and Wright, W. (2017) *Foundations of Bilingual Education and Bilingualism* (6th edn). Bristol: Multilingual Matters.

Ballantyne, K. and Rivera, C. (2014) *Research Summary: Language Proficiency for Academic Achievement in the International Baccalaureate Diploma Program*. Washington, DC: George Washington University, Center for Equity and Excellence in Education.

Barron-Hauwaert, S. (2004) *Language Strategies for Bilingual Families: The One-Parent-One-Language Approach*. Clevedon: Multilingual Matters.

Barron-Hauwaert, S. (2011) *Bilingual Siblings: Language Use in Families*. Bristol: Multilingual Matters.

Beeman, K. and Urow, C. (2011) *Teaching for Biliteracy: Strengthening Bridges between Languages*. Philadelphia, PA: Caslon.

Benson, C. (2014) *School Access for Children from Non-dominant Ethnic and Linguistic Communities*. Montreal: UNESCO Institute for Global Statistics. [Paper commissioned for *Fixing the Broken Promise of Education for All: Findings from the Global Initiative on Out-of-School Children*. UIS/ UNICEF, 2015.]

Bialystok, E., Hawryelewicz, K., Wiseheart, M. and Topiak, M. (2016) Interaction of bilingualism and attention-deficit/hyperactivity disorder in young adults. *Bilingualism: Language and Cognition* 20 (3), 1–14.

Bird, E., Cleave, P., Trudeau, N., Thordardottir, E., Sutton, E. and Thorpe, A. (2005) The language abilities of bilingual children with Down syndrome. *American Journal of Speech-Language Pathology* 14 (3), 187–199.

Braun, A. and Cline, T. (2014) *Language Strategies for Trilingual Families: Parents' Perspectives*. Bristol: Multilingual Matters.

Carder, M. (2007) *Bilingualism in International Schools*. Clevedon: Multilingual Matters.

Carrasquillo, A. and Rodriguez, V. (2002) *Language Minority Students in the Mainstream Classroom*. Clevedon: Multilingual Matters.

Cenoz, J. (2003) The influence of age on the acquisition of English: General proficiency, attitudes and codemixing. In M. García Mayo and M. García Lecumberri (eds) *Age and the Acquisition of English as a Foreign Language* (pp. 77–93). Clevedon: Multilingual Matters.

Cenoz, J. (2013) Defining multilingualism. *Annual Review of Applied Linguistics* 33, 3–18.

Cenoz, J. and Gorter, D. (2019) Educational policy and multilingualism. In D. Singleton and L. Aronin (eds) *Twelve Lectures on Multilingualism* (pp. 101–134). Bristol: Multilingual Matters.

Chalmers, H. (2019) *The Role of First Language in English Medium Instruction*. Oxford: Oxford University Press.

Chimbutane, F. (2011) *Rethinking Bilingual Education in Postcolonial Contexts*. Bristol: Multilingual Matters.

Chumak-Horbatsch, R. (2012) *Linguistically Appropriate Practice*. Toronto: University of Toronto Press.

Cobb Scott, J., Straker, D. and Katz, L. (eds) (2009) *Affirming Students' Rights to Their Own Language*. New York: Routledge.

Coehlo, E. (2012) *Language and Learning in Multilingual Classrooms*. Bristol: Multilingual Matters.

Collier, V. and Thomas, W. (2012) *Dual Language Education for a Transformed World*. Albuquerque, NM: Fuente Press.

Corson, D. (1999) *Language Policy in Schools: A Resource for Teachers and Administrators*. Mahwah, NJ: Lawrence Erlbaum.

Costa, A. (2019) *The Bilingual Brain: And What It Tells Us about the Science of Language*. New York: Penguin Random House.

Creese, A. and Blackledge, A. (2010a) *Multilingualism: A Critical Perspective*. New York: Bloomsbury Academic.

Creese, A. and Blackledge, A. (2010b) Translanguaging in the bilingual classroom: A pedagogy for learning and teaching. *The Modern Language Journal* 94 (1), 103–115.

Cummins, J. (1979) Linguistic interdependence and the educational development of bilingual children. *Review of Educational Research* 49 (2), 222–251.

Cummins, J. (1981) The role of primary language development in promoting educational success for language minority students. In California State Department of Education (ed.) *Schooling and Language Minority Students: A Theoretical Framework* (pp. 3–49). Los Angeles, CA: California State Department of Education.

Cummins, J. (1998) Immersion education for the millennium: What have we learned from 30 years of research on second language immersion? In M.R. Childs and R.M. Bostwick (eds) *Learning Through Two Languages: Research and Practice. Second Katoh Gakuen International Symposium on Immersion and Bilingual Education* (pp. 34–47). Numazu: Katoh Gakuen.

Cummins, J. (2001) Bilingual children's mother tongue: Why is it important for education? *Sprogforum* 7 (19), 15–20.

Cummins, J. (2005) A proposal for action: Strategies for recognizing heritage language competence as a learning resource within the mainstream classroom. *The Modern Language Journal* 80 (4), 585–592.

Cummins, J. (2008) BICS and CALP: Empirical and theoretical status of the distinction. In B. Street and N. Hornberger (eds) *Encyclopedia of Language and Education, Vol. 2: Literacy* (pp. 71–83). Springer Science and Business Media.

de Bruin, A.T. (2015) Cognitive advantage in bilingualism: An example of publication bias? *Psychological Science* 26 (1), 99–107.

De Houwer, A. (2009) *An Introduction to Bilingual Development*. Bristol: Multilingual Matters.

de Mejía, A.-M. (2002) *Power, Prestige and Bilingualism: International Perspectives on Elite Bilingual Education*. Clevedon: Multilingual Matters.

Duarte, J. (2011) Migrants' educational success through innovation: The case of the Hamburg bilingual schools. *International Review of Education* 57 (5–6), 631–649.

Duarte, J. (2015) Cross-linguistic transfer of academic language in multilingual adolescents. In H. Peukert (ed.) *Transfer Effects in Multilingual Language Development* (pp. 221–248). Amsterdam: John Benjamins.

Festman, J., Poarch, G. and Dewaele, J-M. (2017) *Raising Multilingual Children*. Bristol: Multilingual Matters.

Fey, M. and Stalker, C. (1986) A hypothesis-testing approach to treatment of a child with an idiosyncratic (morpho) phonological system. *Journal of Speech and Hearing Disorders* 51 (4), 324–336.

García, O. (2009) *Bilingual Education in the 21st Century: A Global Perspective*. Chichester: Wiley-Blackwell.

García, O. (2017) Critical multilingual language awareness and teacher education. In J. Cenoz, D. Gorter and S. May (eds) *Language Awareness and Multilingualism* (pp. 263–280). New York: Springer International.

García, O. and Baker, C. (eds) (2007) *Bilingual Education: An Introductory Reader*. Clevedon: Multilingual Matters.

García, O. and Kleyn, T. (eds) (2016) *Translanguaging with Multilingual Students*. New York: Routledge.

García, O. and Kleyn, T. (2020) Teacher education for multilingual education. In C.A. Chapelle (ed.) *The Encyclopedia of Applied Linguistics*. doi:10.1002/9781405198431.wbeal1145.pub2

García, O. and Sylvan, C. (2011) Pedagogies and practices in multilingual classrooms: Singularities in pluralities. *The Modern Language Journal* 85 (3), 385–400.

García, O., Ibarra Johnson, S. and Seltzer, K. (2017) *The Translanguaging Classroom: Leveraging Student Bilingualism for Learning*. Philadelphia, PA: Caslon.

García Mayo, M. and García Lecumberri, M. (eds) (2003) *Age and the Acquisition of English as a Foreign Language*. Clevedon: Multilingual Matters.

Genesee, F. (2015) Myths about early childhood bilingualism. *Canadian Psychology* 56 (1), 6–15.

Genesee, F. and Crago, M. (2011) *Dual Language Development & Disorders*. Baltimore, MD: Paul H. Brookes.

Genesee, F., Lindholm-Leary, K., Saunders, W. and Christian, D. (2006) *Educating English Language Learners*. Cambridge: Cambridge University Press.

Gogolin, I. (1997) The 'monolingual habitus' as the common feature in teaching in the language of the majority in different countries. *Per Linguam* 13 (2), 38–49. doi:10.5785/13-2-187

Graf, M. (2011) *Including and Supporting Learners of English as an Additional Language*. London: Continuum.

Grosjean, F. (2010) *Bilingual: Life and Reality*. Cambridge, MA: Harvard University Press.

Grosjean, F. and Li, P. (2013) *The Psycholinguistics of Bilingualism*. Malden, MA: Wiley-Blackwell.

Harding-Esch, E. and Riley, P. (2003) *The Bilingual Family: A Handbook for Parents* (2nd edn). Cambridge: Cambridge University Press.

Hill, A. (2013) The multilingual dividend. *Financial Times*, 3 March. See https://www.ft.com/content/3fd31c1a-85b6-11e2-bed4-00144feabdc0 (accessed 8 March 2018).

Hornberger, N. (1991) Extending enrichment bilingual education: Revisiting typologies and redirecting policy. In O. García (ed.) *Bilingual Education: Focusschrift in Honour of Joshua A. Fishman* (pp. 215–234). Philadelphia, PA: John Benjamins.

International Baccalaureate (2008) *Learning in a Language Other than Mother Tongue in IB Programmes*. Cardiff: International Baccalaureate Organization.

Jernigan, C. (2015) *Family Language Learning: Learn Another Language, Raise Bilingual Children*. Bristol: Multilingual Matters.

King, K. and Mackey, A. (2007) *The Bilingual Edge: Why, When and How to Teach Your Child a Second Language*. New York: Harper Collins.

Kohnert, K., Derr, A. and Goldstein, B. (2011) Language intervention with bilingual children. In B. Goldstein (ed.) *Bilingual Language Development and Disorders in Spanish-English Speakers* (2nd edn, pp. 311–338). Baltimore, MD: Brookes.

Lehtonen, M.S. (2018) Is bilingualism associated with enhanced executive functioning in adults? A meta-analytic review. *Psychological Bulletin* 144 (4), 394–425.

Lewis, G., Jones, B. and Baker, C. (2012) Translanguaging: Origins and development from school to street and beyond. *Educational Research and Evaluation* 18 (7), 641–654.

Lightbown, P. and Spada, N. (2013) *How Languages Are Learned* (4th edn). Oxford: Oxford University Press.

Lucas, T. (ed.) (2011) *Teacher Preparation for Linguistically Diverse Classrooms*. New York: Routledge.

Mahoney, K. (2017) *The Assessment of Emergent Bilinguals: Supporting English Language Learners*. Bristol: Multilingual Matters.

Martin, D. (2009) *Language Disabilities in Cultural and Linguistic Diversity*. Bristol: Multilingual Matters.

May, S. (2008) Bilingual/immersion education: What the research tells us. In J. Cummins and N. Hornberger (eds) *Bilingual Education* (pp. 19–34). New York: Springer US.

May, S. (ed.) (2014) *The Multilingual Turn: Implications for SLA, TESOL and Bilingual Education*. New York: Routledge.

Mehisto, P. and Genesee, F. (2015) *Building Bilingual Education Systems: Forces, Mechanisms and Counterweights*. Cambridge: Cambridge University Press.

Meisel, J.M. (2019) *Bilingual Children: A Guide for Parents*. Cambridge: Cambridge University Press.

Munoz, C. (2010) On how age affects foreign language learning. *Advances in Research on Language Acquisition and Teaching: Selected Papers of the 14th International Conference of the Greek Applied Linguistics Association*. Thessaloniki: GALA.

Paulsrud, B., Rosén, J., Straszer, B. and Wedin, Å. (eds) (2017) *New Perspectives on Translanguaging and Education*. Bristol: Multilingual Matters.

Pearson, B.Z. (2008) *Raising a Bilingual Child: A Step-by-Step Guide for Parents*. New York: Living Language.

Piller, I. (2016) *Linguistic Diversity and Social Justice: An Introduction to Applied Sociolinguistics*. Oxford: Oxford University Press.

Reetzke, R., Sheng, L. and Katsos, N. (2015) Communicative development in bilingually exposed Chinese children with autism spectrum disorders. *Journal of Speech, Language, and Hearing Research* 58 (3), 813–825.

Sears, C. (2015) *Second Language Students in English-medium Classrooms*. Bristol: Multilingual Matters.

Spada, N. and Lightbown, P. (2010) Second language acquisition. In N. Schmitt (ed.) *An Introduction to Applied Linguistics* (pp. 108–123). Abingdon: Routledge.

Spiro, J. and Crisfield, E. (2018) *Linguistic and Cultural Innovation in Schools: The Languages Challenge*. London: Palgrave Macmillan.

Steiner, N. with Hayes, S.L. (2009) *7 Steps to Raising a Bilingual Child*. New York: AMACOM.

Uljarević, M., Katsos, N., Hudry, K. and Gibson, J. (2016) Multilingualism and neurodevelopmental disorders – an overview of recent research and discussion of clinical implications. *Journal of Child Psychology and Psychiatry* 57 (11), 1205–1217.

UNESCO (2007) *Advocacy Kit for Promoting Multilingual Education: Including the Excluded*. Bangkok: UNESCO Asia and Pacific Region Bureau for Education.

UNESCO (2016) *If You Don't Understand, How Can You Learn?* New York: UNESCO.

UNICEF (2016) *The Impact of Language Policy and Practice on Children's Learning: Evidence from Eastern and Southern Africa*. New York: UNICEF.

Waltzman, S., Robbins, A., Green, J. and Cohen, N. (2003) Second oral language capabilities in children with cochlear implants. *Otology & Neurotology* 24 (5), 757–763.

Wang, X. (2008) *Growing up with Three Languages: Birth to Eleven*. Bristol: Multilingual Matters.

Wang, X.-L. (2011) *Learning to Read and Write in the Multilingual Family*. Bristol: Multilingual Matters.

Wesche, M., Towes-Janzen, M. and MacFarlane, A. (1996) *Comparative Outcomes and Impacts from Early, Middle and Late French Immersion Options: Review of Recent Research and Annotated Bibliography*. Toronto: OISE/UT Press.

Index

Academic language, 46, 63, 97
Accent, 13, 17–18, 57, 74
Additive, 27, 42, 44–45
Affective, 42, 68
Assessment, 2, 51, 75, 79, 90–91, 93

Basic Interpersonal Communicative Skills
    (BICS), 46, 63, 97
Balanced bilingual, 16
BICS, see Basic Interpersonal Communicative
    Skills
Bilingual education, 14, 23, 42, 97
Bilingualism, 1–2
    definition of, 7
    benefits of, 7–18
Biliteracy, 52, 97

CALP, see Cognitive Academic Language
    Proficiency
Carder, 7, 45, 49
Cognitive Academic Language Proficiency
    (CALP), 46, 48, 63, 97
Cognitive
    benefits, 9–10
    development, 47–49
Colonial, 8, 24
Communicative bilingualism, 29, 97
Community bilingualism, 2, 21,
    23–24, 97
Community Language School, 53, 75, see also
    Saturday school
Community of practice, 39, 45
Content learning, 53–55
Cummins, J., 46–47

Domains of Use, 41–42, 62, 69, 80–81, 97
Dominant language, 5, 14, 19, 42, 45, 47, 49,
    79–80, 90–91, 97

Early bilingual, 12–13, 61
Employees, 12
Employment, 12
Expat, 26, 34, 70–71, 77

Family language, 11, 21–63, 67–93
Family Language Plan, 1–4, 7–8, 19, 21–63,
    67–93, 97
First language, 5, 8, 12, 14, 18, 22, 24, 27–28, 45,
    52, 80, 97
Functional bilingualism, 34

Gender, 68–69
Goals, 2–3, 21–32, 34–39, 56, 58–59, 62, 65–66,
    72, 76–79, 81, 86, 88, 95

High-status, 14, 22–23, 31, 42–43, 68, 84,
    see also prestige bilingualism, elite
    bilingualism
Home language, 5, 13, 15, 19, 25–26, 40, 43,
    45–46, 48–59, 62–63, 70, 74, 77, 79–81,
    83–84, 98
Host country, 25–26, 98

Immigrant/Immigration, 8, 11, 21–22, 38, 40, 43,
    45, 49, 77, 83, 98
Immersion, 8, 10, 13–14, 25, 30, 37, 42–43, 74, 81
    early, 13
    education, 13–14, 30, 98
    late, 13
Input
    adequate, 16, 23, 33, 42, 67, 76
    enough, 9, 16, 19, 35–36
    map, 36–37
International school, 7, 25–26, 44, 50, 56, 84

L1, 5, 8, 10, 14, 98
L2, 5, 10, 98

Language acquisition, 9, 15–16, 26, 35, 42, 61, 76, 88, 98
Language delay, 26, 28, 89–93, 98
Language status, 22, 43–45, 62, 68–70, 89, 98
Late bilingual, 12–13
Learning difficulty/ies, 4, 62, 88, *see also* learning challenges
Linguistic benefits, 10–12, 56
Literacy, 14, 18–19, 28–35, 49–54
    academic, 30
    basic, 30
    primary, 49–50
    secondary, 50–52
Low status, 43–44, 68, 83

Majority language, 11, 14–15, 17–18, 22, 36, 38–39
Minority language, 8, 17–18, 22, 24, 35
Minority Language at Home (MLaH), 36–37, 40–42, 59, 62, 98
MLaH, *see* Minority Language at Home
Mobile, 21, 31, 71
Monolingual/ism, 2, 4–5, 8, 10–13, 16–23, 25, 31, 45, 56, 60–61, 68, 71, 73–74, 78, 81, 83, 89–93

Mother tongue, 4–5, 18–19, 24, 31, 45, 47, 49, 57–59, 98
Myth/s, 3, 15, 17, 40, 55

One Parent – One Language (OPOL), 17, 23, 37, 38–40, 42, 58–59, 98
OPOL, *see* One Parent – One Language

School choice, 44, 56–57, 66
School language, 5, 13, 41, 44–57, 74, 79, 83, 91, 98
School language policy, 44–45
Sequential bilingual/ism/biliteracy, 12, 42–43, 52
Simultaneous bilingual/ism/biliteracy, 12, 17, 37–42, 52, 71, *see also* One Parent, One Language (OPOL); Minority Language at Home (MLaH); Domains of Use
Social benefits, 12
Subtractive, 27, 45, 98
Summer language loss, 57

Teenage, 13, 38–39, 59, 72, 75, 78, 95
Translanguaging, 18, 37, 54–55, 83–84, 98, *see also* code-switching

Vocabulary, 16–17, 33, 35, 46, 49, 54, 79, 81, 84, 92

Printed in the USA
CPSIA information can be obtained
at www.ICGtesting.com
JSHW050842040624
64245JS00031B/691